AF322592

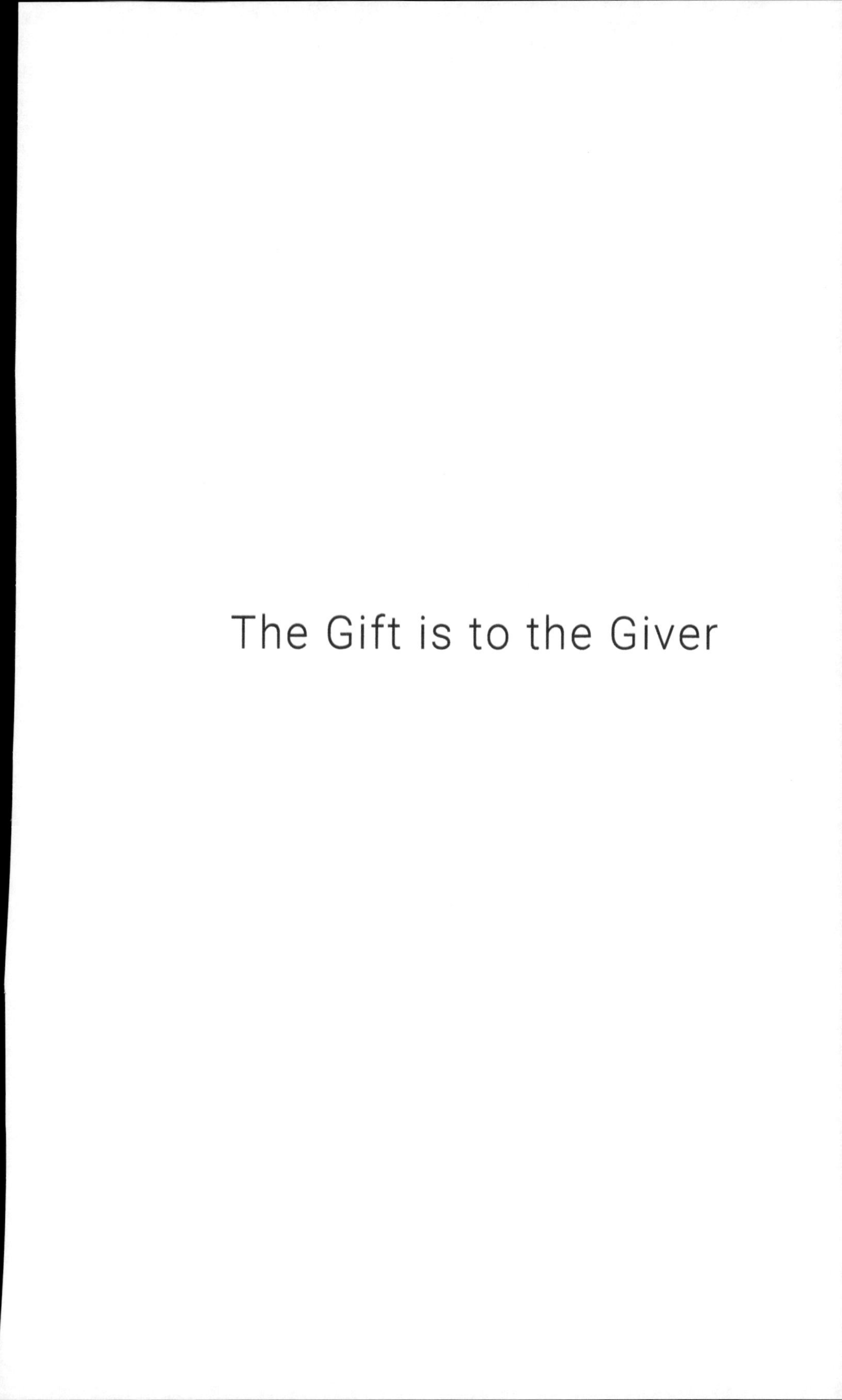

The Gift is to the Giver

The Gift is to the Giver

Chronicles of a 21st Century Decade

Mark Gozonsky

Keppie Usage Publishing

CONTENTS

CONTENTS

CONTENTS

For Dee and Irv

First edition, August 2022 by Keppie Usage Publishing
Copyright © Mark Gozonsky

Versions of these pieces first appeared in *Cauldron* (*"Why Must I Chase the Bus?"*, *"Riding 100 Miles to Citi Field on a Bicycle Built for a Beer Run"*); *Chain Reaction* (*"Orange and Blue at the All-Star Game"*); *Scissors & Spackle* (*"Bike Shoes"*); *California English* (*"Gold Stars"*); *Moxy* (*"The Unfunny Class Clown"*); *Entropy* (*"Remote Teacher Love"*); *EdSource* (*"Reading Gain in an Era of Learning Loss"*), *Lit Hub* (*"Climate and Classroom Change, Parts 1 and 2"*); *The New York Times* (*"How to Teach the Russian Invasion of Ukraine"*); *Statement* (*"The Third Example"*); *City Creatures* (*"House of Straw"*); *Two Hawks Quarterly* (*"A Voyage of Self-Discovery, Not a Maelstrom of Self-Loathing"*); and *The Sun* (*"Gritty All Day Long," "The Orange Appreciation Award," "How I Got to First Base"*).

Library of Congress Cataloging-in-Publication Data

Gozonsky, Mark, 1961 -
[Essays, Short Stories, Selections]
The Gift is to the Giver: Chronicles of a 21st Century Decade / Mark Gozonsky
ISBN 979-8-218-04793-1 (print) -- ISBM 979-8-218-04795-5 (E-book) 1. Happiness 2. Reciprocation

The gift is to the giver, and comes back most to him—
it cannot fail;
The oration is to the orator, the acting is to the actor
and actress, not to the audience;
And no man understands any greatness or goodness
but his own, or the indication of his own.

Walt Whitman, "Carol of Words"

I am my own favorite writer. Then comes Shakespeare. Then Cervantes. I want Alice Munro to be on this list. Bob Dylan, obviously way up there. As Bob once said to Leonard Cohen, "Leonard, you're number one."

To which Leonard replied, "If I'm number one, what number are you?"

Says Bob, "I'm number zero."

The methodology for my own ranking is, how much of an author's stuff I've read. I am *way out ahead* based on this. I am a copious re-reader of my own stuff. I find the rhythm of it reassuring: the bip and the bop.

And I like it. Getting up in the morning, writing three pages. Having an idea and following it where'er it doth lead amid the furrowing folds of my brainpan and out into the world beyond.

Which is where we meet. Howdy! Thank you for being here. This collection does not include every single thing I have ever written. That would be a lot! It is a mélange, as we like to say on Gozonsky Farms, of things written between 2012 and 2022. The through-line as I see it involves chronicling how an everyday fellow such as myself actually goes about the business of being the change one wants to see in the world. Amid climate change and Trumpism and #BlackLivesMatter and COVID and all the general bleakness and dark-side -- how, particularly for a person who is upbeat by nature, do you check the box of

___ I'm a good person.

The response entailed herein involves teaching, gardening, bicycling, and ruefulness (mostly about errant throws). There is consternation, certainly, even alarm, as well there should be. Yet when I read over this stuff, the main impression I get is bouncy-bouncy-bouncy-bounce. I think that uplift is part of the gift offered hereunto. Naturally, anything you like is yours for the taking.

I also want to say I have learned something. Many things! For one example, in the essay "House of Straw," it's obvious I have no idea how to round up a flock of chickens. Now I do. Show up with a cup of chicken feed. A canister of oatmeal will also work great. Shake it! Oatmeal in a cannister makes a great percussive sound. You could use any seed or grain, really. Mealworms, too. So long as you make it obvious you're going to feed them, they'll follow wherever you go.

Fair Harbor, New York
June 30, 2022

Bicycle Sagas

1

Why Must I Chase the Bus?

Why must I chase the bus? Has the instinct been passed down from some hunter-ancestor who chased down gazelles across Ethiopia three million years ago? That has to be it. Our spirits all once inhabited built-for-speed bodies so dark they glowed like the moon in daylight. Feeling humanity's common ancestry in my hamstrings is one of the many benefits of trading the lead back and forth with the 733 Express on my bike along Venice Boulevard from the Westside to downtown L.A.

Another benefit is demonstrating the willingness and ability to tear out with all my might as I accelerate ever-more-rapidly through my mid-fifties. Since time is flying, I'm flying with it, in bright orange bike shorts and a black helmet round as my dad's old bowling ball; always on the lookout for discontinued low-end Toyotas and any white car whatsoever. In my experience, these are the cars to beware. They are so prevalent that if you beware of them, you are essentially ready for anything.

When the green light hits, I stand up, lean forward, and crank through the 32-lane intersection at Venice and Sepulveda, hip-shaking, boogie-ing, hoochie-coochie-ing and classic rocking to beat that long red bus which might be going twice as fast but also has to stop twice as much. The race is really not so much against the bus as it is against the lights. If you keep making the lights, you'll be fine.

Thing is, you can't cheat and run the red. You also can't fake right at the Brazilian mini-mall or Dr. Boris's plastic surgery storefront and then pretend like *oops, I really meant to be going straight*. Such behavior is flagrantly unsafe, and even if you think you're getting away with it, you're setting a bad example. There could be kids around. Bike-cheating also erodes your competence as a driver on those occasions when you have no choice but to take the wheel. There is no doubt I drive like I'm riding my bike, therefore I must obey traffic laws while pedaling — despite the temptation to behave like a white Tercel. My ethical jukebox says *don't don't don't don't do it*.

Such non-stop deliberations have the additional benefit of making the commonplace uncommon. I have traversed Venice Boulevard to and from downtown L.A. in the upper hundreds of times, potentially enough to render it routine, but bicyclists cannot afford boredom. Take your surroundings for granted and soon you're recognizing how the street looks not only black but also many different kinds of blue and even silver on impact.

Fortunately, the bus race keeps me connected. To my red, black and white road bike, to the scenes whooshing by: people waiting outside the carwash with their skateboards and shopping bags and hope; billboards for Marley-brand weed, proclaiming the truth that "Herb is a plant" and the untruth that "It is good for everything"; the strip mall festooned with trapezoids as though designed by a child on the very first day she ever tinkered with building blocks; the triangular park outside the Actors Theater with the vast oak trees and sprawling homeless population; the fish place on Culver proclaiming "Yes! We Have Gumbo on Fridays!"

Everything is a milestone. A few days ago I chased the 733 even though it was nowhere in sight. The benches in front of the carwash were empty, so I must have just missed it. It had to be up ahead, that strawberry-red double-long bus with the crinkly part in the middle like the bendable part of a twisty straw. I chased it past the billowing white flowering pear trees — which you can always count on to start L.A.'s jubilant procession of flamboyant ornamentals — past the vast power grid at Fairfax, past the Rosedale Cemetery at Normandie, beyond the mortuaries in the shadow of the 110 freeway. Chasing a bus that wasn't visible felt like pursuing a distant goal — in my case, getting a book published, or graduating from college for the high school students to whom I'd be teaching English at the end of my ride. Just because the 733 was not visible didn't mean it was not there, which I suppose is how many people feel about believing in God.

For an hour and five minutes, pumping as hard as I could, even through the flats between Crenshaw and Arlington which lull you into complacency, being ever so slightly uphill, enough to make you think, "Oh, what's the use?" I declined the flats' invitation to complacency just as you're supposed to be able to decline depression's invitation to feel horrible about everything. The fact is I never caught up to the 733. It was a snow leopard, a quetzal, but the fact is also that I never gave up.

The bus is my obsession, but it is not my nemesis. On the contrary: we are partners in the struggle against cars. Cars, especially single-occupant cars, are the nemesis. Someday my grandchildren are going to ask me, "Grandpappy, what did you do about climate change?" I look forward to being able to look them right in their clear, impressionable eyes and tell them about how the bus was and still is my second-favorite way to get around.

I always sit in the way-back where no one can creep up on you, and make friends by asking people who are blaring their music what we're listening to. They are always so happy to turn it down a little and talk music with you. That's how I got to know Big Sean and Lil Reese. People who blare their tunes on public transit really just want someone to notice them, and since I am possessed by an otherwise rare gregariousness when bus-riding, I'm only glad to oblige. The 733 takes me out of my head, and also to my favorite places: the Central Library, my high school, Dodger Stadium. The 733 and I are friends.

And yesterday I beat it, helped by a cyclist thin as a palm frond who whipped past me at Vermont while I was feeling good about being in the lead. Many times this same guy has been a neon green plastic jacket flapping past me and gone. Today, however, we kept pace up to the stoplight at Hoover, where I could see he had a few drops of runny-nose juice mixed with another few drops of blood pooled below his nostrils. Like something a hummingbird would sip.

I asked him if he had any cycling goals. He said yes: to ride to work every day. That's good, I affirmed. He asked me about mine and I told him about the bus, which at that moment pulled up behind us like the shark in *Jaws*.

"I get it," he said, and we zoomed off, him especially. Without his flat-out pace I might have lagged, but he was with me. So I sped beyond my limits. I gave it a few of my best Bruce Springsteen huhhhs and blew that bright red bus away.

Victorious, after an entire day feeling great about it at school, stashing happy little pieces of joy in all the lockers up and down the hallway — the top lockers, and the bottom lockers, too — I cruised the whole way home, admiring the billowing white flowers of those dependable, buoyant pear trees. They start at St. Andrew's Place on the edge of Koreatown. I wonder where they end.

2

Orange and Blue at the All-Star Game

My bike and I make the train to the All-Star Game with no time to spare. This is a recurring pattern. I always assume everything is going to work out fine. I assume so adamantly, aggressively, in defiance of the hovering idea that perhaps I might actually enjoy looking into doing just a little bit more planning.

It's a reaction against my people's inherited penchant for worry. My particular people are Ashkenazi Jews conditioned to worry by centuries of pogrom. I mention it right here at the start because earlier in this racial violence-filled summer of 2016, W. Kamau Bell said in *The New York Times Magazine*, "When the 'good white people' of the left won't claim their whiteness, they think they're doing a good thing, when they're actually opting out of America's biggest and most defining problem." I don't know if being Jewish counts as being white, but I do know I want in: in on the struggle to overcome racial violence, and in on the baseball All-Star Game.

I'm taking my bike on the Metro Liner south from Union Station in LA to Oceanside, 40 miles up the coast from San Diego, site of this year's pageant. Whited-out graffiti on the concrete embankment of the LA River turns to non-whited out graffiti on the sides of industrial buildings abutting the tracks headed southeast from downtown. There is industry aplenty in LA — smelting, concrete mixing, feather-cushion making — more making, storing and shipping of regular normal things big and small than we media-minded Angelenos typically dream of.

Personally, I am dreaming of a seat in the upper deck behind the catcher for $300. That is the going rate as of last night, and the amount my wife — determined to live within our means while saving for retirement — has set as my budget. I plan to perch up there and soak in the pastime, not so much rooting for any particular player but rather basking in the game itself. While rapturously recalling Carl Hubbell's five consecutive strikeouts of future Hall-of-Famers in 1934 while admiring contemporary mound wizard Chris Sale's ability to toss whiffle ball curves using a hardball, I will also interview fellow fans about this summer's dreadful police brutality and revenge killings. Since we are already there to be part of something bigger than ourselves, these conversations will further transform the annual celebration of baseball prowess into... I dunno, but am determined to find out.

The problem is that cyclist mode and interviewer mode don't really gel. In cyclist mode you're pretty much whir, zip, cool, gone. Whereas in interviewer mode, you linger. The best answers frequently come when the formal interview itself is over. Cyclists gotta keep moving. Thus on my bike ride from Oceanside to San Diego the only human interactions I have are:

1. A very short and slender man in a straw hat who asks me for a dollar at the sundrenched Oceanside train station so he can get a Bailey's and Cream;

2. A lean older gent on a green touring bike who utterly smokes me on the also sundrenched 101 South in Encinitas, pausing only long enough to ask if orange is my favorite color and when I ask how did you guess he ha-ha's and says it's very visible;

3. An easily-startled guy in Solano Beach who flinches when I announce "On your right" while passing him and the grocery bags dangling from the handles of his mountain bike. I vibe with the waves crashing on the beach until that same guy and his groceries pass me going uphill in Del Mar;

4. An entire crew of cyclists who leave me in the dust climbing the Torrey Pines grade without a word except from the one woman at the very end who says, "I'm going to try to catch up, wish me luck." I do and it works because soon she is out of sight while I continue to create my own rain from the sweat dropping off my bike cap. It is rare for anyone who doesn't look like a greyhound to pass me in LA but this is what happens when you surrender home field advantage.

5. A beatific kid standing under a tree in Mission Bay Park who looks up from his phone to exclaim, "I just caught a Pokémon." I tell him, "That's what I figured." What I should have said was "Congratulations" but you cannot get these snippets of bike conversation back. They're like the last line of Robert Louis Stevenson's poem "From a Railway Carriage" –

      Each a glimpse and gone forever!

6. If there ever was a guy to talk to about these troubled times, it should the guy in the huge NY Mets-emblemed T-shirt walking a similarly huge dog on the Rose Creek Trail, a pastoral patch on the San Diego outskirts, where Wordsworth and Coleridge would have been happy to discuss the merits of having the All-Star Game determine home field advantage for the World Series. Yet at the moment of truth it turns out he's just a kid and what am I really gonna say — "Hey kid, is there a race war going on?"

No. Like a good Angeleno, I have to polish my pitch. And so instead of human interaction, I settle for breathing in the fresh-cut outfield lawn of the exquisitely rendered diamond at the Mission Bay Athletic Center. And that is sweet, but not what the times require.

I will say that human interaction-wise I have a grand time Snapchatting all the way with my daughter in Chicago. I snap her my perspiration rain forest in slo-mo and she snaps back herself and a friend transformed into bumblebees.

Such moments help me carry my daughter in my heart but we all carry our loved ones in our hearts and that alone will not turn back the tide of race hatred in America. Like Van Morrison sings in "St. Dominic's Preview," we got to get outside of ourselves. At least I think that's what he's saying. Is it actually "get outside empty shells?" In any case, in downtown San Diego old rivals do seem to be reconciling. Fans from all over the country root together old school, the Carlton Fisk 27 Red Sox jersey walking side-by-side with the Tony Perez 24 Reds jersey amid a throng of Tony Gwynn Padres19s.

Oh yes I want to be in that number -- although of course our All-Stars aren't saints. After a couple of especially disheartening revelations about domestic abuse and non-payment of child support by Mets players, I had asked my beyond-expert friend Bryan to restore my faith by naming at least three Mets known to demonstrate good character. He came through in the clutch, texting back more than ample documentation that David Wright, Noah Syndergaard, and Curtis Granderson all give back plenty. This keeps my faith alive, but even amid San Diego's All-Start pageantry I can't quite summon ga-ga hero worship.

This is also because all of the "affordable" seats on SeatGeek that were there last night are gone goodbye an hour before game time — another miscalculation in my miscalculation column. Not even in my most flagrant financial recklessness could I shell out $500 for an "Awful Deal" on SeatGeek and expect a hero's welcome at home. Therefore I shift into Plan B – watch the game from a bar and engage my fellow patrons in conversation not only about pennant races but even more so about racial justice in America and the lack of it and what to do.

Unfortunately, whizzing past people for four and a half hours has rendered me somewhere on the spectrum between marginal and invisible. For example, at the Starbucks closest to Petco Park, where I sit down with reviving banana and replenishing almonds at a big empty table, a guy wearing an orange tie and two All-Star caps, one on top of the other, sits down next to me.

"You're rocking the double-cap look," I complimented him sincerely. It's easy to tell I'm sincere because I am wearing two hat-like accoutrements myself, a bike cap and helmet.

"I am rocking it," he retorts, pivoting nimbly to his phone. Fine. Time for me to run an errand, get another notebook. Look at me, running errands on my bike in a completely different city from the hometown I woke up in earlier this very day. Anything is possible — anything!

Feeling the snacks kick in, I exclaim "Nice socks" to a guy crossing Island Avenue with orange socks pulled up to his shins. He keeps right on crossing rather making friends.

Not a quitter, I exclaim, "I like that shirt" to another my age-ish guy sporting a Mark Fidrych jersey and Tigers cap outside the Albertsons on 14th Street.

"Thanks," he says, and nothing more.

I have always taught my students that saying "Thanks" and nothing more is exactly how you're supposed to respond to a compliment, yet in this case I find it disappointing. I want Detroit to open up to me about how profoundly the legendary free-spirit Mark Fidrych influenced his life: by making it okay to talk with open passion with inanimate objects such as baseballs; okay to make ardent love with your heart's delight on the precise site of your life's most significant places, such as the Tiger Stadium pitcher's mound. But no. Detroit is intent on his destination, not up to chat with some random sweaty cyclist. Thus discouraged, but unbowed, I start looking for a bar.

At the Half-Door Brewing Company, seated at a four-top by myself with a cheeseburger, fries and superdank IPA in front of a television the size of Temecula; center field at Petco is 200 yards down the street and crowd noise is not just tipping pitches but telling the future in advance of the two-second tape delay. I could not be happier unless my dad had been lobbing 'em into me at the Home Run Derby. In fact, it feels like we have already done that and now my late father and I are together admiring all those Red Sox, his favorite team, in the starting lineup for the American League.

The All-Star introductions are my very favorite part of the game. I ultra-love it because one or more players inevitably write Hi Mom on the brim of their cap or on their palm -- except none of them do that this year. So since I've already taken imaginary BP with my dad, let me pinch hit for all of the 2016 All Stars and say Hi Mom right here.

Hi Mom! I had a blast texting with you during the game. Yeah, Eric Hosmer does kinda have Frida Kahlo eyebrows. Yeah, it's too bad that neither Max Scherzer nor Paul Goldschmidt are in fact Jews. No brethren in the game at all this year, but last year we had Ryan Braun and Joc Pederson. Next year in Miami! OK! Love you!

As it turned out, my mom was my only friend during the game. There were other patrons at adjoining tables, but they had their own conversations to attend to. I was that weird guy sitting by himself, doing both play-by-play and color commentary out loud for the audience in his head.

ME: Very noble of Canoe to work that walk.

ME: Shows discipline.

ME: Yes.

On the way back to LA, the Amtrak Surfliner has to rescue a broken-down train ahead of us between Santa Ana and Anaheim. It can't in good faith not rescue it. Still, the delay means getting home to my wife not at a tolerably late hour but in some undefined dark category of way-beyond lateness. And here I had made it to the station in Old Town San Diego with time to spare for a *salsa verde* burrito, only to have the train enter a time warp in which the shaggy-looking guy sitting across from me keeps bumping his head on the overhead rack every time he gets up to adjust what looks like his wordly possessions.

He has a story to tell about how he had sold everything he had in Seattle and come to San Diego to look for his long-lost sister, but he doesn't insist on talking about that. He'll talk about anything. At long last here's someone I could ask about race in America, but now I'm too busy worrying how to get home when the train finally rolls in to Union Station, long after the last bus has come and gone.

I could just ride the 12 miles home. I do it all the time in the daylight and often enough after Dodgers games, but we're talking dead of night here. The prospect of heading down into the Metro at 7th and Hope doesn't thrill me either. I'd be very vulnerable carrying a bike down those urban stairs.

Option three: pick up the bus at Spring and 7th. Or is it Spring and 6th? The schedule I'm consulting is vague, and so I keep on worrying until the train gets in so late that unless I ride the whole way home through the scary dark, then I have catch the bus.

Bike lights flashing, I ride down Spring Street past the homeless encampment across from City Hall. It's bracing to see all those tents and feel all that sleep-breath in the air, except from one tent where a woman is raising a ruckus. I wonder if she is the same woman who earlier in the day had been explaining to amused-looking construction workers something cosmic, slowly and deliberately, like pouring out the bottom of a jar of honey.

That cosmic woman was certainly the friendly homeless person I used to give leftover Breakfast in the Classroom apples and cheese sticks to in Grand Park after school. She always accepted these offerings with thanks. Then we would talk about other things, such as the weather, or about vampires versus werewolves and which are more dangerous.

"They're both equally bad," she calmly assured me. I missed a day or a week delivering our leftovers and then hadn't seen her again until today.

My rear light blinks while shooting out red laser beams on both sides, creating my very own motorcycle-esque escort.

"Nice light," says one of the many Black guys waiting against the front of the long-closed Tierra Mía coffee shop on Spring and 7th. This particular Black guy is about my height, skinnier but not too skinny in a similar way to how I'm burly but not too burly.

I'm so glad to finally have someone to talk to.

"Thank you," I say. Together we admire the red lasers blinking on the pavement. "You create your own path," I add, meaning it as a product endorsement. The guy repeats these very words – "You create your own path" -- and taps his heart. We're brothers!

Another guy asks, "Are those lasers?" This is an older, browner guy, standing closer to the curb. I roll my bike over and give him a demo.

"I've never seen that before," he says, in the tone of a person who has seen many things and values fresh perception. He is wearing yellow-tinted aviator glasses, a blue down jacket and a Dodgers cap. He goes on softspokenly to tell me that he had just arrived from Seattle on the train, and also that he has been sober since 1975.

Rather than exclaim, "That's the year *Born to Run* and *Blood on the Tracks* both came out!" which my heart is thumping and yet I sense might not interest him, I ask, "What turned things around for you?"

He tells me he had drank so much that he required an operation on his pancreas. Then, a month later, he drank so much again that he required a second operation on his pancreas, this one after blacking out somewhere between Seattle and a VA hospital in Phoenix.

"Did you ever find out how you got to Phoenix?" I ask. He shrugs.

"How does anyone ever get to Phoenix?" I say to put him at ease. Putting us both at ease is a man whom I have often seen and heard at that precise corner, blasting oldies from a homemade rig, not a boombox, with speakers the size and shape of soup cans set up on top of the garbage can. One hot day a year or two ago he was blasting "Black Magic Woman" and it sounded so perfect, the apotheosis of Santana.

Tonight I ask him, "Is that the Del-Fonics?" The song has that delicate balance between doo-wop and soul, but he gives no reply. I consider my follow-up question while eyeing his two bicycles, because there is only room on Metro buses for two bikes and he was plainly here first.

A large woman spanning the corner of the building itself seems to be offering a discography but upon more focused listening wants two dollars for food. Although I had earlier in the day happily given a dollar to the guy in Oceanside, I do not immediately fork over the cash. A rabbi once told me that if someone has reached that place where they're asking for money, it's graceful to fulfill their request. This same rabbi — shout-out here to Zoë Klein! — also once said that when you stop a car to let someone cross the street, it's like stopping a tank that could crush them.

The problem at Spring and 7th at 2 am on July 13, 2016 is that opening my wallet in this particular here and now seems like it could be a rookie move. This is not the ideal place for the flashing of the cash. So I demur and hang back against the wall like everyone else, feeling relieved when Santana packs up and rides off with both of his high-handled-bar'd bikes. He gets off to a rickety start because he also has to balance his soup can speakers, but by the middle of the inter-section, going the wrong way against traffic and also running a red light, he finds his rhythm and is gone.

"You admire that," observes my new friend with the yellow-tinged aviator glasses, who I hadn't realized is standing with me.

"It's hard to ride two bikes at once," I reply, hoping I might now be on a streak of street-corner preaching if he touches his heart to affirm the inner truth of my proclamation, but he demurs. Instead he asks if I'm hot.

"You're the one wearing the down jacket," I think but do not say. He shares further details regarding his train journey that I miss out on due to the persistent explosions of long-past 4th of July firecrackers.

Amid all this excitement, along comes the bus. I put my bike on the clunky, non-intuitive front rack like a pro while everyone else gets on and then there at the bus door is my original friend, the heart-tapper. I imagine we'll sit together in the way-back and discuss whiteness and blackness and Jewishness and togetherness but instead I wind up next to my other new friend, the older, browner guy from Seattle

We proceed to have a downtown-to-just beyond Culver City con-versation that starts with his reason for being in LA, which is to preside over a funeral. He is a spiritual leader of an Indian tribe centered 60 miles (good bike-riding distance!) north of Seattle. Tribal medicine is in his family, going back to the 1400s. He knows this because of stories told on totem poles and talking sticks.

"That's a long time for wood to last," I observe.

"It's cedar," he explains, adding details about the preservation pro-cess. He introduces himself as Daniel Half Moon and says he has a several centuries old eagle feather in his beat-up roller suitcase. I am about to ask, "What are its powers?" but figure its powers must involve what one makes of them. Instead I say, "It must be very fragile."

"It's a great responsibility," he clarifies.

The woman in front of us has her own beat-up roller suitcase on the seat next to her and is adamant about keeping it there, so much so that she refuses a gentleman with a Spanish-from-Spain accent who asks if he can sit there. She makes him sit next to a great big gender-uncertain sleeping mass with a hood covering their entire head and taking up a seat and three quarters. The Spanish-accented gentleman perches on the edge of the seat, uneasily.

Meanwhile, the woman in front of us, who is wearing a badge holder not for All-Star game credentials but from Bad Boys Bail Bonds, gets a jar of Vaseline out of her roller and begins applying it liberally to her face. She admires her shining reflection in the bus window of the night. The guy on the edge of his seat pulls out a bottle of wine to share with his own new friend, a young man with exquisitely rendered eyebrows and short shorts. This new friend made a sour face when he tastes the wine.

"*No le gusta*," I Spanish-simulcast to the sommolier.

"That's because it's 100% wine," he replies. "Too good."

He shows me the bottle and it is my absolute #1 wine favorite, the Coppola Claret.

We do not all party down together however, because it is time to ask my question about race relations to Daniel Half Moon. I formulate it the best I can, although it is not exactly the question I was originally inspired to ask by Keeanga-Yamahtta Taylor in *From #BlackLivesMatter to Black Liberation*, which I had thought of bringing with me in my backpack on this trip but had opted instead for *The Wandering Jews* by Joseph Roth.

The question I ask Uncle Half Moon (calling an Indian leader 'Uncle' is a sign of respect, he had told me) is, "How free can we be in America?"

I imagine he will reply, "What do you mean by 'we'?" and I'm ready: "We the people." But instead he looks at his hand as though reading his fortune. Then he tells me that America is a much more diverse place than it was back in 1975. People who have come to this country since then need to have their own stories told. They also need to have the process of voting explained bettter, because it's very confusing. This is the essence of his answer. Access to indigenous stories and to voting determine how free we can be in America.

He continues to answer beyond the question, saying that humanity has at most 25 years to stave off environmental apocalypse. Somberly he says, "The birds are confused by air pollution. The butterflies are confused. Most important, the bees are confused. They're confused about time. When you confuse insects about time, you're near the end."

So are we. We reach my stop at three-thirty in the morning. Daniel Half Moon and I bid farewell and the oenophile gratefully takes my seat. I wonder what they'll talk about! Meanwhile, I check in on my sleeping wife, then stay up for another hour, writing the bus conversation down. I wake up with my wife, make her coffee, and keep on writing.

Since then, I keep checking the baseball scores like always, hoping against hope that the Mets will win despite the dismaying tendency of their best players to suffer season-ending injuries. What's different since the All-Star game for me is, I have asked my how-free-can-we-be question and gotten an answer. It's a streak of one, infinitely better than a streak of zero.

3

Riding 100 Miles to Citi Field on a Bicycle Built For A Beer Run

Do-able math excites me. Fifty miles there, fifty miles back. There being Citi Field, home of the New York Mets. Back being Helene and Kenny 's house in Ocean Beach, southeast from the ballpark ... across half of Queens, all of Nassau County and into Suffolk County, plus a 30-minute ferry ride across the Great South Bay to Fire Island — home of my wife's favorite childhood memories.

Fifty plus fifty equals a hundred miles, also known as a bike marathon or "century" in cyclist talk.

Three weeks ago, I completed a century around Lake Tahoe. It's no big whoop. I ride about 25 miles round-trip from work most days during the school year. On the Tahoe ride, I was tagging along with my wife like a dog chasing after something — like a car, but not a car. Even if I was a dog, I still wouldn't love cars. Point being, my wife rode her own century to raise money for cancer research, and since I tagged along with no undue side effects, the Fire Island to Citi Field century seemed mathematically plausible.

There are likely to be some potential complications — which, by nature, I do not so much ignore as disdain, like Diana Nyad swimming from Havana to Key West without a shark tank. First of all, I'm not taking the ferry. You can't take your bike on the ferry, which settles it right there.

My wife suggests renting a road bike where the ferry docks, in Bayshore. But while my wife understands many, many things, she does not get the folk art appeal of using the materials at hand, which in this case consist of Helene and Kenny's old lady's-style beach cruiser, black in color, with a wire basket, rusty bell, balloon tires, one speed, coaster brakes and not-too-rusty chain. Perhaps she does not understand the appeal because I have made no effort to explain it, which I really ought to do if I want my life partner to understand the real me, because riding 100 miles on a bike designed for a beer run feels like destiny.

"It would be considered a limo in rural China," is the extent of my briefing to my wife. I know this from reading *Iron and Silk* by Mark Salzman many years ago, yet still remembering vividly the scene in which his beater bike is the object of envy from all the rural Chinese he encounters.

"Rural China," my wife repeats, perhaps hoping to offer cognitive behavioral therapy. Instead, I take it as consent. At the time, neither one of us knows that Salzman compares being able to buy his choice of models at a bike shop in Changsa to being able to walk into a dealership in the U.S.and pay cash for a Porsche. Also, Changsa is hardly rural. At the time of his 1986 memoir about traveling to China to teach English and learn Kung Fu, the local population exceeded one million residents.

Still, nobody is real-time fact-checking me at this stage of life. What we can know for sure is, the New York Mets are playing the Kansas City Royals in a much-lower-stakes replay of last year's World Series — in which the Royals systematically clobbered the living embodiment of my childhood.

Furthermore, my best friend Jimmy is meeting me at the game with his wife and their two sons. We have spent many summers together flipping baseball cards and eating ice cream at their house in Western Massachusetts, where Jimmy still listens to the Mets on WOR, fading in and out on his transistor radio. In real-time, it is patently urgent and important that I rendezvous with them after riding from Fire Island to Flushing on this beach cruiser.

In this way, the journey is compelling because it is so quixotic. The corroded beach cruiser is clearly my Rocinante. Also, rather than squander the fund-raising potential of riding a century, I have invented a noble purpose: Raising money to aid Fallujah refugees, whose plight in sandstorm-swept 110 degree Iraqi heat feels important while my toes bask in Fire Island's soft cool sand. The faded Mets cap I am wearing instead of a bike helmet is palpably our deluded hidalgo's *morrión simple,* or a simple cap, albeit made of steel as opposed to cloth.

If you told me here in my hometown of Los Angeles that I would be planning to ride a century in a baseball cap instead of a helmet, I would surely tell you that's crazy. This, in fact, is how my wife characterizes my plan to everyone with whom she speaks — our daughters, her parents, her sister, my mother. I unhesitatingly interpret this as her pride in my willingness to dream the impossible dream.

I even have a Dulcinea, in the sense that me and Jimmy's best-friendship hinges largely on the romantic momentum still pulsing from that first half of the 1988 season we shared as baseball reporters for a now-defunct San Francisco alternative weekly. Those few days of actually hanging around the batting cage and unabashedly rooting in the press box are shimmering light from an ever-more-distant star.

Nevertheless, on our birthdays and through baseball-seasonal communications on Opening Day, during the All-Star Break, and the day after the World Series, we continue to follow that star. Furthermore, our friendship transcends utter fantasy. I went 2-for-2 on attending his son's Bar Mitzvahs; and he came to my twin daughters' B'not Mitzvah as well as to my father's funeral. So I would have to give myself the edge over Don Quixote in the sense that my romantic ideal has a stronger foundation in reality than his completely deluded love for Dulcinea.

In most other senses, however, it's a close call.

The journey starts at 5:28 am on June 22, 2016. For the first thousand yards it is steady rolling, with dawn's early light behind me and adventure ahead. This adventure will consist especially of trans-something my upbringing: born on the 16th of July, 1961 in Booth

Memorial Hospital, 2.2 miles from the site of what will soon become Shea Stadium, the Mets' first ballpark, where my dad and mom will drive me and my sisters from our green house in East Meadow, in the middle of Nassau County, to watch Tom Seaver and Cleon Jones lead one of the all-time great improvements in proficiency, as the Mets go from hapless misfits to World Champions within the span of my first eight years.

Mine is not a childhood that needs to be transcended any more than every else's does: not in the way that Diana Nyad's stated desire to overcome childhood sexual abuse motivates her 100-plus mile swimming marathons; nor in the way that children who are currently refugees from Fallujah will need somehow to transcend their experiences of war. What my Queens-to-Nassau County childhood most needs trans-something-thinging is its ever-greater distance from the moment we call now.

And in the present moment of 5:32 am on June 22, 2016, the pavement of the Midway in Ocean Beach gives way to sand at the western edge of Corneille Estates. From here I "must" portage the bike a mile and half over sand. This is pleasant insofar as I like scrub pine and the scenery here feels like being in a paradoxically larger-than-life bonsai garden. Birdies chirrup on obsolete telephone lines; the waves pound out their steady vigil in protest against ocean pollution, a vast wrong that the ocean as we all know is rising up against.

This is one reason why riding a bike to Citi Field is not crazy. Driving a single-occupancy automobile is crazy. Yet people do that all the time. It's the normal crazy, like owning slaves used to be.

Such are my thoughts whilst trudging, which quickly induces a full-body sweat and yearning for asphalt. A mile-and-a-half trudge does not bestow full Lawrence of Arabia-hood; nor do I seek it, because I am content with being quixotic. Nevertheless, I do welcome pavement when it reappears next to a grass-like tennis court in Dunewood. From there it is smooth-as-the-end-of-*E.T. the Extra-Terrestrial*-cycling all the way to the Fire Island lighthouse. Yes, to the lighthouse, black and white as a cow, standing in a meadow, blinking to signify that everything about home-is-the-sailor, home-from-the-sea and Virginia Woolf's trans-somethinging of her own upbringing is, in this moment, safe and sound.

And yet, here is where the journey's troubles begin. Not to blame Google Maps for my own foolhardiness, but, I blame Google Maps for my own foolhardiness. Google Maps says not only that I can ride my bike all along the Midway's impassible sands but also that I can roll across the Robert Moses Causeway, connecting eastern Fire Island to Long Island. This is in fact not do-able, and also not a surprise. Most people I have consulted have been firm in their certainty that no bikes are allowed on the causeway. However, since Google Maps plus one guy at the hardware store where I bought spare inner tubes said sure, go for it, I am going for it — right up until I see very clearly the No Bicycling signs posted on the bridge. There is also a nice man in an orange vest holding up a sign directing the open lane of traffic.

He tells me, "Sorry, I can't let you go" as I stand there, apparently forlorn.

"That's all right," I say. "I can read the signs."

But can I really? It is not so much that I absolutely must ride my bike over this bridge. The nonexistent shoulder of a single narrow lane over an eight-mile expanse is not a position from which even I in my neon Mets-orange shirt want to lead the parade. However, I do want to continue my journey, even though the obstacle that seemed pretty well confirmed yesterday when I called the Robert Moses State Park and the ranger said no, you can't ride bikes on the causeway and you wouldn't want to anyway because "people tend to drive crazy on it."

Even I with my blue-and-orange sneakers and knee-high orange socks can imagine them driving extra-crazy if a dude on a coaster was hogging the one open lane. So out goes Plan A, to my chagrin. This chagrin is not as great as it used to be, back when I was totally Plan A or Bust. This change must have settled upon me sometime during my career as a public school teacher; probably in the latter, more-successful phase.

For Plan Bs I had:

- B1) Hitch a ride over the bridge;
- B2) Wait for the bus to Babylon that a guy told me about near the Lighthouse when he too said I couldn't ride over the bridge; and
- B3) Turn back, abandon the bike and take public transit.

B3 was out of the question not so much because of obstinacy but because a police officer cruising by on the Robert Moses State Parkway had warned me I couldn't ride my bike on it, not even on the shoulder. I know — the sound of da police is da the sound of the beast. Nevertheless, on those extremely rare occasions when a cop tells me not to do something, I am loathe to do it again. This is perhaps one part of my upbringing that could use some transcending. Meanwhile, run-ins with the law are where I draw the quixotic line, so the thrill is gone from riding my bike on the parkway.

Plan B1, hitching a ride, is also out due to the Chris McCandless rule; which is, whenever you are on an outdoor adventure and reach a decision tree, do the opposite of what you think Chris McCandless would do. The anti-hero of *Into the Wild* did things like burn all of his money; abandon his car (that, I can relate to); and hitch rides all across the US from Arizona to Alaska, resulting in a destiny I would prefer not to spoil in case you have not yet experienced that book and that I would even more prefer not to share.

My hitch-hiking aversion is also intensified by having recently read "A Distant Episode" by Paul Bowles, in which perhaps the all-time most hapless misadventurer very quickly reaches a do-I-keep-going-or-should-I-turn-around point in what turns out to be an excruciatingly ill-conceived plan. He rationalizes that "he ought to ask himself why he was doing this irrational thing, but he was intelligent enough to know that since he was doing it, it was not so important to probe for explanations at that moment."

After reading that story, you know it *is* important to probe for explanations. It really, really is! Therefore, I probe and determine I am riding my bike from Ocean Beach to Citi Field because it seems like more fun to ride a bike for five hours than to sit on public transit for two and half; and also, because at the age of almost 55, I want to show the world — as represented by my Facebook friends as well as everyone who glimpses me en route in my neon orange Mets shirt — that I still can.

Hence the clear preferability of Plan B2. Wait for the bus. Keroauc did it. He starts *On the Road* by misguidedly hitching a ride north from his aunt's house in Paterson, New Jersey to Newburgh, New York. He hopes to follow Route 6 — "one great red line across America" — only to discover in buckets of rain with no shelter that Route 6 does not go through to Chicago. After "crying and swearing and socking myself on the head for being such a damn fool" he has to take the bus back to New York and start over again, which he doesn't even bother to do. He just takes a bus clear to Chicago.

If the bus was good enough for Keroauc, it's good enough for me. *Babylon by Bus* is my favorite Bob Marley album. None of its tracks come to mind, though. In fact, I will have no songs in my head for the entirety of this ride. I am here and now, even during the hour and a half it takes for the S47 bus to roll up at just after its scheduled time of 9 am, still on June 22, 2016.

When the bus arrives, I secure Rocinante to the bike ramp and enjoy the ride, chatting with the scalp-shaved bus driver about how he likes about the job — "It's a career-type job with its ups and down like everything else" — and living on Long Island — "It's hard to leave; it's surrounded on all sides by water."

The southern part of that water of glistens and ripples, ripples and glistens. When prompted, the bus driver suggests taking Jericho Turn-pike until it turns into the Northern Parkway and following signs for 25A. That would be a straight shot, but over coffee and a scone at my first SAG at Jack Jack's Coffee House, I consult Google Maps and see this will cause me to overshoot East Meadow. It is clear to me now that East Meadow is my true destination, the place of my bike-riding youth, yes, on a metallic orange Stingray with a banana seat. Here I will inter-sect in place and if not in time then in mode of transportation with my youth. The graph of these coordinates must needs be determined, by me, today.

Indeed, that is my destiny.

In the parking lot of the CVS, where I pause for sunscreen and Payday bars, a man whom I imagine to be Haitian speaks what I imagine to be Creole to someone somewhere else. After this pause for provisions, the miles roll away. Blue and yellow wildflowers roadside in East Massapequa; ducks on a pond in Wantaugh. Not merely cruising but power-cruising, elbows and forearms resting on the bars, hands clasped, mighty mighty hamstrings pumping away. A big wide long truck pulls up beside me. The passenger sticks his thumb up. They're pacing me!

At a stop sign I ask, "What am I doing?"

"Twenty!" he says.

"Right on," says I, despite suspecting their odometer is not perfectly calibrated. "I'm going to Citi Field," I share with Whitman'esque delight in my fellow man.

"Not riding, I hope," says the driver.

"Heck yeah," says I.

Out comes the passenger's thumb again. That's two thumbs up. "Stay hydrated" says the driver, in that Long Island accent, as if spoken through vestigial gills gurgling up an additional W for Water on certain vowels, depending on the tide.

I do stay hydrated, otherwise stopping only to post selfies. At Newbridge Road I'm at the outskirts of my known childhood universe. Richie the freckle-faced kid on my Little League team lived way out here in Bellmore. We might have practiced on that very field I'm passing right now. On Merrick Road the nursery school me and my two sisters went to goes by in a blur. Let it. It's not nursery school I'm after. Past Jerusalem Road, past North Jerusalem Road, paths forever paved in my neurons from sheer repetition and redolence, yet without any sense of direction. Little kids don't know where any road is going, but I know where I'm going. I'm going to Prospect Avenue.

Prospect Avenue Elementary School no longer exists. It was torn down and paved over in 1978. Speaking of paving, they are doing some kind of deep road-scraping on Merrick Road. This forces me up onto the sidewalk, yes, riding on the sidewalk, exactly like a kid. Cedars and maples have uprooted this sidewalk, turning it into a perpetual launching pad. Fine with me. I have balloon tires. I can fly!

At Prospect Avenue, I stop to make a proclamation. Perhaps I am not as hydrated as I should be; certainly my face is smeared with sunscreen. Nevertheless, it feels altogether fitting and proper to express my exuberance. I tend when overjoyed to bust out in Spanish and here I go:

> *¿Quien está viviendo el suuuuuuuuuuueño? Yo 'stoy viviendo el sueño. Eso es la calle de mi escuela primaria. Lo se fue pero ya yo soy aquí.*

Who's living the dream right now? I imagine myself to be saying. I'm living the dream right now. This is the street my elementary school was on. It's all gone but I'm still here.

I post this rant on Instagram and no one likes it except for Don Quixote.

After that it's a corn muffin with peanut butter at the Apollo Diner, where suddenly it's noon and there ain't no way I'm making it to Citi Field by bike for a 1 pm start. You know how I hate having to go to Plan B so I take a little time letting reality sink in. I won't be riding all the way to Citi Field, no, not today. At a Dominican restaurant called Dominican Restaurant on Front Street in Uniondale I hit the Uber button and four minutes later Kamruzzaman rolls up in a shiny black Escalade.

I have mixed feelings about Uber'ing it. On the one hand, the entire impetus for the journey was to go see the Mets with Jimmy and his family. Conceivably I could have pedaled all the way, but in that scenario would would arrived very late in the game. That is not being a good friend. Sometimes you have to set your personal narrative aside.

And replace it with sports! Thor was somehow hurling 98 mile-per-hour sinkers despite a tender elbow. In a well-played game of dueling dingers, the Mets prevailed, 4–3. Nine innings was hardly enough time for me to catch up with Jimmy and family; long enough only enough to be with them, together, root-root-root-ing for the home team.

I Uber'ed most of the way home, too. What was supposed to be a hundred mile ride turned out to be more like 17, maybe 19 if you count the portage over the sand. Taking the 7 subway, I got as far as Woodside and 60th, only to determine that the bus I was supposedly going to take wasn't going to be happening because the none of them had bike racks. Theoretically I could have pedaled back, but it was already almost six and the last ferry to Ocean Beach left at 7:30 sharp. I absolutely did not want to miss it and be exiled from our vacation home.

Enter Safiullah and his dusty Honda Pilot on Roosevelt Avenue, where the subway running overhead had me discombobulated. I nearly told him about my giant hurry before recovering some manners and saying hello, introducing myself and asking him how his day was going. This got us off to a much better start. We discussed the various exigencies and agreed on safety first. That settled, I straight-out asked where are you from, and he said guess.

I guessed, "Right here in Flushing."

He said, "How did you guess?"

"We have a lot in common," I told him. "For example, right now, we're both headed for Bayshore." But really, I guessed Flushing because this xenophobia has got to stop, right? And you know: be the change.

It turns out he was a translator and language instructor in Afghanistan for the U.S. Army. They brought him over here, but now that the U.S. is out of Afghanistan, there's not much need for intensive instruction in Pashto and Urdu. Hence, driving for Uber. He loves America because of the security and education for his three children. In 35 years of living in Afghanistan he never experienced 40 back-to-back days of peace.

Everybody learns from their Uber driver. This is the way it should be. I guessed his name must have something to do with Allah and he said yes, it has multiple meanings: blessed by God, chosen by God, slave of God.

By the time we got to Bayshore with no minutes to spare, we were close. I said my best to you and your family and he said the same to me, touching his heart.

4

Bike Shoes

No one has passed me on my bike in the two weeks since I got bike shoes. This is a big change. Before I got bike shoes, little kids on tricycles passed me. The tortoise from the Aesop's fable "The Tortoise and the Hare" passed me. I would say to myself, "Sure, but they are not carrying 30 pounds of computer and books on their backs," but secretly, I knew that the weight of my high-school teaching gear was not a good excuse. They were passing me because I was slow.

Being slow is not the worst thing you can be as a bicyclist. The worst thing you can be as a bicyclist is in a pool of your own blood on the side of the road.

The point is, theoretically, I have no problem with going slow. I understand slow's upside. Our contemporary life is too hectic already. Nonetheless, I hate it when people pass me. I want to leap from my bike, onto their backs, drag them off their bikes, and kill them.

Is this wrong? So be it. I don't have to worry about snapping like that now, because now I am exactly like Mercury, the winged messenger of the Gods. We both wear helmets, and we both have wings on our feet. I feel immortal, invincible, except for the suspicion that my body is gradually being colonized by my hamstrings and quads. There is a possibility, even a likelihood, of my becoming a five foot eight and a half inch thigh if I don't seek out both humility and companionship.

The humility should not be too hard to come up with. Truth to tell, there is one guy who has passed me in the last two weeks. Deep down, I knew someone would, some Olympic athlete or Tour de France type. Professional bicyclists and tri-athletes are exempt from my competitive mania, and this guy fit the profile. He was riding a Cannondale, wearing an I. Martin bike shop shirt. He did not need to be riding a multi-thousand dollar bike nor wearing a shirt from LA's snootiest bike shop for me to identify him as an Olympic caliber bicyclist, because I had already decided that anyone who passed me on my bike immediately qualified for the Olympics. There will be others, I am sure of it, and I will chase them like a dog chasing a car, until they're out of sight and I can return to my fantasy of being the fastest.

I think companionship is also within reach, although it's complicated. The reason I say that is, bikes are not made for talking to people. You're on your bike, they're on theirs, and you're both supposed to be pedaling away, looking to make sure no cars are coming, thinking your own thoughts, which is something I'm good at and like to do as much as I can, usually by myself.

The exception here is my bike-riding friend Len. He writes me really short e-mails to see if I want to go riding. The entire e-mail is in the title. For example: "Ride Saturday?" I admire his brevity and try my best to imitate it. I write him back: yes! or, no! Len is a short-named man, even shorter-named than I am, yet conversely much, much friendlier. In fact, one thing I treasure about him is how many people he knows, including many bicyclists, a couple of whom have joined us on our forays, which thus far have advanced as far south as the tip of the Palos Verdes Peninsula and north up to Leo Carrillo State Beach, the one with the tide pools.

I once took my daughters up there to see the tide pools when they were in one of the tide pool grades, 2nd or 3rd, and I will always remember this guy playing Frisbee by himself. He was hurling that disk into the offshore breeze, and it was hurtling back to him like fate. He was stripped to the waist, hungry-lean, long straight haired and straggly-bearded, chanting outer-space language, permanently on acid.

"That is not me," I stated matter-of-factly to myself, although I have played Frisbee with myself. It was right before my daughters were born. I would go to Lindberg Park in Culver City and run the same drill as the dude by the tide pools. Hurl that Frisbee with all my might and scamper madly after it. Maybe that's how he and I were different. The guy at Leo Cabrillo was firing bullets right back to himself; my solo Frisbee heaves required me to take off after them, as if I were my own pet retriever.

It was an odd time of life for me. My wife and I were trying to conceive, we were still pretty new in Los Angeles, and I must have been lonely. Later, after the girls were born, we'd take them to that same park in Culver City. In fact, that's where we met Len. He was playing with them in the sandbox, with his own even younger boys nearby. They were getting along great. He has a knack for people, Len does. He communicates interest in your well-being. For instance, he recently criticized my use of coffee as a bike-riding liquid. He said, "Everything I've read says coffee dehydrates you over the long run."

I thought, "You are reading too much of the wrong stuff," but I also thought, "Thank you for caring about what I drink. That's what my father would do if he could."

When you get to be my age, very few people offer you precautions. They either figure you know what you're doing or are waiting to enjoy their well-deserved *Schadenfreude* when you get your come-uppance. That is the essence of comedy, so I don't blame them, but I do find it touching that Len cares what I drink, and the truth is, recent weeks have found me starting to switch out my daily big bottle of frozen coffee for a big bottle of water.

"Uh-oh," I think to myself. "I am becoming a bike-shoe wearing water-drinker." I told you there were many changes going on. Truthfully, I think less is more on the coffee and more is more on the water.

Our bodies like water and I like having clearer pee. It's instant evidence that I am being a virtuous person.

Another change I like since getting bike shoes is the change of my bike route to and from work. I have rediscovered the Ballona Creek Bike Path. The best thing about it is that it is like being in a dream, hurtling down a path with no impediments, just flow. There is actual flow. A shallow, broad creek is running alongside you, glinting and rippling. Various birds skim the surface. There is no need to know their names. They are birds, like faces in a dream. You are hurtling, and that's the important thing. You can think things, not think things, it doesn't matter, all the time you are propelling yourself along, twisting and twerving but mostly just hurtling. Essentially you have become your own heart, pumping and pumping, and pumping.

Teacher Tales

5

Gold Stars

A giant hand came out of a big puffy cloud and pointed its giant index finger right at me. Then a voice so deep it shook the ground said, "You there! Yes, you! Become a teacher."

I was standing, when this happened, in the office of my daughters' soon-to-be elementary school. The roof must have suddenly parted so I could see the finger pointing down from the sky, but otherwise it was just your average elementary school office. Lots of beige. A tissue box. Some flowers that looked confused about where they were. But I was not confused. I was where I wanted to be, among the helpful ladies in a room full of paper with a counter in the middle so you knew which side you were on.

The office ladies' kindliness appealed to me because this was a time, Spring 2001, when my happy career as a writer and editor for a hyper-booming internet company (which I'll call I4M) had turned, upon my promotion into middle management, into a ping-pong marathon between isolation and redundancy. The less creativity I got to express at work, the more energy I put into volunteering at my daughters' school. I felt appreciated there, especially by Claire's kindergarten teacher, Mrs. Beckett. The reason stars appear to twinkle is not because of atmospheric conditions, but because of the radiance emanating from Mrs. Beckett's teaching.

I did a lesson involving drawing a barren tree from standing at the trunk and looking straight up. This was during my last winter at I4M, when I had the feeling that all of the trees with no leaves on them would never have leaves on them again.

"Bravo!" said Mrs. Beckett. "These kids need to learn how to look at things differently." I read Degas and the Little Dancer to the class, and then had the kids pose for one another and do observational drawing. How they teetered on their toes! The seriousness of a first grader drawing a classmate who has one arm akimbo, the other arm gesturing off, off to the future, a future that must remain benign for as long as they can hold that pose: that was seriousness far more riveting than anything I encountered at work. Mrs. Beckett told me, "You should be a teacher." I took this not as an off-hand remark, but as necessity.

I was soon propelled towards this fate by being let go at I4M. My wife took it well. She was certain I could find another great job within the month of severance allotted me. Her confidence might have been oppressive if I did not have an equal confidence of my own, powered by two clear goals. One, to prove to my wife I could not get any job other than becoming a teacher; and two, to not just sit around feeling it was my destiny to become a teacher but to actually become one.

To fulfill the requirement of seeking a non-teaching job, I asked my daughters what they thought I should do next. Claire said I should work at an art museum; Lilly proposed an amusement park. I networked in those fields, the result of which was an essay I sent to *The Wall Street Journal.*

It did not publish the essay but did include me in an article about non-traditional job search strategies. A few months later, Oprah's producers got wind of it and tried to get me on the show, but by then I had already gotten a teaching gig and was way too busy to return their calls until they had already booked the segment on Dads Who Live Vicariously through Their Daughters.

I got my first teaching job so quickly because this was the second-to-last year of anyone who wanted to become a teacher being able to go right ahead and do just that. Imagine going to the airport and deciding, "By gum, I have had it with the same-old same-old of merely being a passenger. Today I have a notion that I would like to try my hand at flying one of these impressive machines." Immediately, along come representatives of the Aviator Induction Commission in their blue blazers and shoulder epaulettes, hustling you through security and into a cockpit, where they point out many of the buttons to you before wishing you good luck and reminding you never, never, never to push the red one. Or is it the blue one? You'll find out soon enough.

Such a thing could never happen. And yet: that method was good enough for the California Commission on Teacher Credentialing. I got three weeks of cramming on classroom management (Post the classroom rules where everyone can see them!) and lesson planning (Do lesson planning!) And that was pretty much it, except for three days when I watched some experienced teachers treat their students thoughtfully.

One of them in particular, Ms. Leonard, sat a frightened-looking boy in the front row and whispered encouragement to him. Whenever I have had a child in my class who either looked frightened or who frightened me with the notion that I would not be able to reach him, I have sat him in the front row and tried to whisper to him like Ms. Leonard. Sometimes these whispers are just thoughts in my head, but they echo her inspiration to be a thoughtful, caring teacher. I wish I had had more time to observe her.

I'd like to say my mother inspired me to become a teacher, because it's true that her thirty years as a much-decorated elementary school art teacher do inspire me. However, it's even more true that my mother was specifically set on warning me against something I was just as specifically set on ignoring.

She kept saying, "Teaching is very demanding." It's not really like her to speak in such short sentences, unless there's a lot she's not saying. I listened with my "What she's really saying is that she loves me" translator turned up full blast, so that instead of picking up on any nuance hinting that I might not be up for some or all of these demands (as it turned out I definitely would not be, try as I might, for at least five years) – I just heard the Paul Simon song, "Loves Me Like a Rock."

This overabundance of confidence and optimism is one of my favorite personality defects because it comes from a lifetime of basking in my parents' love. A big reason I became a teacher is to be an aqueduct of love, passing it along from my life into the lives of my students. This is a nice idea; however, in practice, love in teaching is like meat in sausage, requiring extensive processing -- reflection, assessment, planning, collaboration; as well as personal attributes such as stamina, consistency and self-forgiveness -- before it can be safely consumed. Otherwise, you're just sitting up there at the front of the classroom in your altruistic broth, and to your students, you look just like a giant clam, something seemingly inanimate, with a big smile, easily broken.

The extent to which I have figured any of this out, I largely owe to my father, who has passed along to me at least some of his formidable power of not being a quitter. This was most impressed on me when we did yard chores together and he came in an hour after I did. It was further impressed on me by the boxes of carbon copies I recently sorted through, containing eloquent, succinct cover letters after he got let go from his job the year before my older sister started college.

It has always seemed to me that having made the mid-career switch, I was also responsible for making good on the decision. While I do think that sense of duty comes from my father, I also feel, when I look back on the moment the finger pointed down at me from the sky, that the deep voice wasn't telling me to be like my father, or mother, or any other teacher I had ever known.

It was telling me to be like myself, the way I was in the fifth grade, working at my desk, getting gold stars from Mrs. Carson. She had a chart showing everyone's gold stars. I don't recall having the most, but I do remember having a lot of them. I was a presidential biographer in the fifth grade. I could tell you what Tippecanoe and Tyler Too meant, who Lemonade Lucy was, which presidents were famous for failing at other jobs before occupying the Oval Office. Reciting their names in order, from Washington to Nixon, gave me a feeling of the scope of history. In the fifth grade I could know, do, be -- anything. What inspired me to enter the teaching profession is to feel that way again.

6

The Unfunny Class Clown

I let Damian do his project on serial killers in Iowa. This seemed like a bad idea, which was the point. It was early March, end of school year in sight, and Damian had been having bad ideas since August, when we wrote about imagining what we'd be doing a year from now. His answer was 'Selling oranges by the side of the road.'

In classroom discussions, he liked to tell his friends, 'You're stupid.' He also liked to seize on incidental use of words such as 'roll' or 'ingest' as opportunities to intimate his recreational use of marijuana, by snickering.

The oranges scenario I kept to myself for personal worrying. Low self-esteem of that magnitude can't just be pep-talked away. What to do, though? Hmmm. I wanted to think of Damian as someone other than the unfunny class clown, the saddest clown of all. When I asked him after class about un-positive contributions to our learning environment, he would apologize with flagrant insincerity, looking like a big bad wolf who intended fully to blow down another house as soon as our little talk was over. He had the wolf's wet grin and overzealous gleam, as if he knew the brick house and boiling kettle awaited so he had better get his damage done now, yet also knew his story would be told in perpetuity and therefore he would always return to power.

The thing to do when your students start reminding you of fairy tale villains is call home, yet I never did because amongst my flaws as a high school English teacher is assuming that the kids who irritate me the most cannot possibly have a competent parent, or else why would they be behaving so badly.

Furthermore, school has an institutional bias against badness which I personally resent. The rules and rhetoric all postulate a world of un-relenting goodness which relegates badness to places of shame instead of recognizing its status as an essential element of human nature. Yet report cards and attendance awards and pep talks do not ensure good-ness among students, or faculty for that matter.

For example, not all of my own ideas are splendid. Oh, not hardly. There is one bright, talented girl in period six who shakes her head vehemently to indicate no-no-no whenever I draw near. She is a sober individual with several college scholarships awaiting. The simple fact, which you could get right or wrong on a test, is: my way is not hers.

Yet still I approach the bright, talented, not amused girl. I am not a giver-upper. Maybe this time is the time the well-meaning gesture will be accepted. She will not leave the gold star on her desk, crumpled like a wounded starfish.

__ Maybe.

__ Don't count on it.

__ But still: if you're a teacher and you've given up, it's time to heed another calling.

I have not given up. Just the opposite. I am the right amount of zealous in the interpretation of problems as opportunities. For exam-ple, I view the girl who shakes her head no as a reminder of my need to connect with people more straightforwardly.

Damian, who wanted to do his project on serial killers of Iowa, has the exact same problem – or else the opposite problem, of being too straightforward. My inability to get a read on him was obvious from Day One, in August, when we were illustrating words that called to us from poems that spoke to us. I had borrowed umpteen poetry collec-tions from the downtown library: beatbox poets, Sufi poets; poetry of all the lands and peoples. The surefire, can't-fail, perfect first day lesson goes like this:

1) Find a poem that speaks to you,
2) Identify a word that's calling,
3) Write and illustrate the word big and bold,
4) Include enough lines for context,
5) Give the meaning, and
6) Explain why you chose it or it chose you.

Craving, defiant, indelicate, lamentation, cosmic, queer, impenetrable, nameless, illuminated, immense, destiny, adamant, millenium and essence were among our words.

Damian's word was 'Fuck You.'

He ran it by me, first, supposedly wanting to make sure it was okay. In a sense, it was him being, ha-hah, watch me say f-u to the teacher and get away with it; in another sense, it was me thinking, ah-hah, here's a young soul to work with from the get-go. So I told him, sure, go ahead. But after some uncharacteristic after-thought, I posted all the kids' words from all of my classes except for Damian's f-u, simply because I didn't feel like looking at it all day long. If he wants to get his work posted, let him come up with and follow through on something more original.

Yet even though we began each class with compliments and good news to get a good vibe started before I make kids put their phones away, Damian continually lobbed crude insults at his pals – that's stupid, you're ugly – in a braying, I-hate-myself tone that further challenged my motivation to somehow try to build this kid up within my jurisdiction of reading, writing, listening, speaking and the fuzzy zone of 'being nice to people'.

Despite all of my pedagogic derring-do, however, Damian remained committed to his flinching, cringing, meant-to-be but not-funny, instead maddeningly irritating mode of discourse. This is not to say he wasn't bright. One time when we were discussing literary elements he asked whether a phrase could combine consonance, assonance and parallel structure.

'Sounds poetic,' I ventured, attempting not to hope this was The Breakthrough. 'Do you have an example?'

'Yes I do,' he announced with the stagey aplomb of a seasoned talk show guest. 'Poison semen.'

'Bingo,' I said, using breeziness to disguise my feeling that Damian was a kid needing more help than I had to offer.

Iowa turns out to be fertile soil for serial killers. We were studying it to figure out how this swing state voted for Trump in the 2016 election. Before you seek to be understood, seek first to understand, and things of that nature. John Wayne Gacy and Jeffrey Dahmer both lived for significant stretches in Iowa. I really did not want to know any of the factoids Damian was promptly uncovering, such as that Dahmer's father possessed an advanced degree in chemistry.

All that schooling and look what happened.

Yet, on the plus side, while researching Iowan serial killers Damian was engaged and productive, which I could tell because he was writing things down in a remarkably clear handwriting that looked like it was continually turning cartwheels.

Also, I had a new theory. The presumably feigned interest in serial killers and all the negativity in general was a cover-up for the lovingkindness Damian felt deep down but feared ridicule for exposing. Somebody must have made him uneasy about showing kindness, which is sad. He had it in him, but where? If you can't find it in the light, you have to look in the dark.

If I only could endure this exposure of serial murderers' biographical material. They weren't always and exclusively killing people. That came After. There has to be a Before when they do the same stuff as other people. Have a busy father. Have a missing mother. Go to school. Get in fights. The more Damian excavated about serial killers' distinctive ghastliness, the more widely opportunities would emerge for him to express his own authentic gentleness.

This was the theory.

Well, as I said, it was a bad idea. The more Damian uncovered about Iowan serial killers, the more he smiled – not a healthy, prime-of-youth smile, but rather a hang-dog simper. This I could not endure, so one day while all the other teens were working on their Iowa agriculture, Iowa music, Iowa fashion, Iowa food, Iowa maps, Iowa monuments, and Iowa memes exhibits, I called Damian to my desk for a sober assessment.

'How are you doing?' I asked, feeling proud of my desk. Earlier that day I had cleared it off so now there was room for his elbows should he decide to make himself at home.

'I'm doing Wunderbar,' Damian stated with patently false glee, pronouncing the W as a V and elongating the r beyond endurance. I listened with my liver, which told me that the glistening in his great big eyes predicated shame.

'Glad to hear it,' I replied, feeling my words mean their opposites, and also feeling us about to plummet as though we had arrived at the apex of a badly maintained amusement park free-fall. To fend off panic, I got to the point.

'Stop working on serial killers,' I told Damian. 'Work with Mathilda on fashion.' That was it. No little jokes. No hoo-ha. Just me telling him what to do.

His gleam abated yet still remained alarming, decreasing only from about 180 to 140 percent of what I would consider roughly normal.

'Yes, sir,' he said. Did I detect a note of sincerity? Within that note, was there a quaver of gratitude for being set on the proper path?

Mathilda is a powerful figure in our classroom, preternaturally composed yet adolescently buoyant. Both of her parents are pediatricians and they raised a healthy child. Mathilda emanates bodily well-being. This newly decreed partnership between her and Damian would be a peer-to-peer intervention for the ages. Come witness the healing power of peer-to-peer intervention, I beckoned the misty legions of imaginary teachers whom I want to impress with my smoothness.

Sure enough, Damian and Mathilda were soon huddled together, elbow to elbow. I toured the room murmuring approval, bestowing big checkmarks. When the bell rang, everyone turned in their work so it wouldn't evaporate into the papersphere – except not the normally clockwork Mathilda and her new sidekick Damian.

'Let's see what you got,' I insisted, bursting with pedagogic swagger based on two factoids gleaned with a glance at another kid's map of Iowa lakes and rivers. Iowa has 132 lakes and 25 rivers. This was something at least one of my students demonstrably knew. The system was working.

'We're not really finished yet,' Mathilda demurred.

'Finishing is overrated,' I plunged ahead.

They exchanged 'oh well, he asked for it' glances, and then from the deep recesses of her purse Mathilda produced a sheet of spiral notebook paper, incompletely de-fringed, with three or four jagged lines that looked drawn in hard dirt by a burnt stick.

'I'm having a hard time making that out,' I said, my vision blurred by a welling up of the ducts reserved for tears of frustration.

'It says most Iowans dress like the Donner party,' said Mathilda, in her home-made Southern drawl, the result of a not-quite-yet-over childhood imagining herself as Disney's Black Princess of Alabama. Normally I find this accent as adorable as the dictates of my profession will allow, but now it induced a ringing sort of shrieking in my innermost ear.

In his braying voice, Damian elaborated, 'The Donner Party, you know? They ate each other.' He spoke in highest spirits, as though describing a rager I could have been invited to but wasn't.

'The transcontinental cannibals,' I assured him. I once read a whole book about the Donner Party, westward pioneers from the USA's covered-wagon days who died so excruciatingly, it was as if they had been especially designated by fate to pay for the sins of manifest destiny. I actually finished it, which is uncommon for me; I'm much more of a skimmer-browser-set-asider. Something about the painstaking methodology of their archaeologically-recreated suffering spoke to me, although now I can't remember anything except that those poor souls moved extremely slowly in their duress – unlike Mathilda and Damian, who exited briskly, speaking what sounded distinctly like crowd chatter in a play, leaving me to confront yet again the fact that good kid never upgrades bad kid. It's always the other way around.

Clearly it was time for me to resort to one of teaching's most power-ful strategies: leave the kid alone. Not solitary alone, facing the corner; just alone as in temporarily separated from the warm power of your good intentions. Teens are very change-able, and often a youngster with a personality disagreeable to you will pop up one day with a whole new, much more copacetic iteration they dreamed up all by themselves while you ministered elsewhere.

Therefore, instead of continuing to squint at Damian, I turned my attention to Savanna, a 9th grader with immaculate cornrows whose progress over a semester and a half consisted of a) sitting in her assigned seat and b) easing up slightly on her hissed running commentary of my lessons, which differed from that of other classroom dissidents by consisting not of irrelevant juvenilia but rather of pinpoint accuracy. Instead of calling me out under her breath as she had earlier in the year, each time I ventured some bit of not-wisdom clearly not-destined for the Pedagogy Hall of Fame, Savanna was now mouthing her tally silently to herself. This was progress of a very unsatisfactory sort.

Yet in retrospect it seemed like the Golden Age of Athenian Democra-cy. Somewhere around March, Savanna had worked loose of her self-restraint and moved on to nonviolent resistance. She would slouch as if spilled over her desk, with fresh clean sheet of paper completely blank, and her book upside down, backwards and out of arm's reach. When I raised my hand for attention, she would allow her inner monologue to become just sub-sibilant enough to register protest. When I raised my eyebrows, she returned the favor with an expression most dour, like a cat refusing spoiled milk.

The convenient explanation for such non-compliance is that the student must be sTooopiD, but Savanna's reading scores, while low, were not heart-wrenchingly low. They told me Savanna got the message but refused to accept it.

I might have been able to respect her integrity and leave it at that, except I also remembered glimpsing, within the crook of her elbow, a fragment of early-in-the-year autobiography that read '...behind bars and I will be too....' I don't know if she actually wrote this or if I made it up after observing how stiffly she walked during her frequent bathroom and water breaks. She moved rigidly, with exaggeratedly even steps, as though she had learned to walk in shackles.

The thought came to me that Savanna's non-compliance was a hunger strike. She was simply not gonna take it, in which 'it' stands for the whole rotten deal. Truth, again: this was not the first time I had the hunger strike idea. It reoccurs to me every so often when faced with a flat-out non-compliant kid who reads well enough to read the writing on the wall.

This time it occurred to me while talking with her learning lab teacher, who was about to present findings on Savanna to the committee. Typically when the hunger strike epiphany occurs, I think, 'Hmmmm' but this time I thought, 'Pudding.' As in, go to the store, get a few different flavors of instant pudding so that one is bound to be one she likes, save up a bunch of milks from Breakfast-in-the-Classroom – and then employ pudding as a lever to move the world.

While mixing and shaking and watching the fixings congeal, Savanna and I would bond.

I got this idea from reading a college friend's brother's social media post about what you would say if you could say anything to Trump. My answer was, 'Mr. President, let's make some pudding.'

Thus, a few days after Damian and Mathilda presented their findings about Iowa fashion and the Donner Party, I bestowed boxes of vanilla, chocolate and caramel pudding upon Savanna along with the big bag of half-pint milks and bright plastic containers we would use to shake things up. She smiled broadly, looking delighted. Then, with a free and easy smile, natural as the divine spark within us all, the girl I always knew was hiding back there declared, 'I don't eat pudding.'

I swept it all away with one forearm swoop into the black hole-sized garbage bag I had on hand for the mess! Also, I did not lash out at her non-miraculous response to my out-of-the-box thinking. Instead, I dutifully got back to haranguing the other kids about the global refugee crisis.

Her learning lab teacher says she's going to recommend Savanna move to a different school where they have smaller classes and receive more individualized instruction. This sounds euphemistic to me, like sending a bad dog to a farm. It'll be sad to see her go, but you can't argue with 'I don't eat pudding.'

During this break from attempted mind-controlling of Damian, I still continued observing him. One morning he held a door open for me and my bike. That was undeniably nice. I also spotted him sporting some Guatemaltecan drawstring pants, comfy-looking and colorful. I went through a big Guatemaltecan textile phase in my late twenties. Sometimes it can be annoying to recognize commonality, as in, when you think you're higher/mightier than someone and it turns out you're not, but I also can't argue with the comfort and color of Guatemalan textiles. And sure enough, shortly thereafter, Damian finally did something good in class. I asked, 'Who has a steady hand with a video?'

Damian alone volunteered. He who had held the door open for me and my bike. Who had turned to serious-eyebrowed Priscilla, after Priscilla declared she would be spending Saturday night with her boyfriend, to say, 'Oh Priscilla I didn't know we had made plans,' which I thought was actually funny and also gallant.

Damian who had tripped gaily up the hallway, dancing and a-prancing, hand easily in hand with another boy who led him like a prize goat at a 4-H fair. That was pretty dainty.

Damian who now presented himself as being ready to take a video of me urging advocates of undocumented students to call their senators in support of an urgently needed piece of legislation facing the do-the-opposite-of-whatever-is-good policy of the current administration.

As unstable as our president is, so is the camera on this video steady. We got it in one take and afterwards Damian said, 'You're a natural.' This made me think camerawork could be a plausible way for Damian to express his individuality professionally.

So I asked Damian to stick around for a quick minute after class, and – unlike many thus summoned students, who bank on my forgetting and slip away unnoticed at the bell – he presented himself front and center at my desk, looking unprecedentedly at peace with himself, as though his inner gong had been sounded and now hung perfectly still.

'That video you made was really good,' I told him.

'Why thank you,' he replied. 'I took a community college class in video composition and got college credit, so that's all taken care of.'

'Great,' I told him, gladly taking solace in the words college and credit. 'Camerawork can be a good way to earn a living. I remember at the start of school you predicted that you'd be selling oranges by the side of the road, and that has been worrying me.'

'Well, how kind of you to follow up,' he said as though all along he had the manners and wit of Oscar Wilde. Then he finished me off for good. 'I was having a bad day that day. I'm really not planning to sell oranges by the roadside. I'm planning to study creative writing.'

7

Remote Teacher Love

Teaching under any circumstances, dire or otherwise, is largely about holding back. You love your students, of course. That's a prerequisite. It's a very high-level, conceptual love, a Knights of the Round Table type of thing, involving good deeds—*not* the piercing falsetto love of love songs.

Teacher love also doesn't last. It used to bother me how eleventh graders vanished into twelfth grade, never to be seen again. Now I look at eleventh graders as annual flowers, such as cosmos and zinnia. Sunflowers, too. Loveliness incarnate. They last as long as they last and that's that. If you want to experience those flowers again—delicate stems, fierce color, mathematical elegance—you have to plant new seeds, which is like getting a new class of students.

I had one former eleventh grade student, two years ago, come in at lunchtime shortly after the start of twelfth grade. She announced it was her birthday and that we were having lunch together. There was no discussion; it was fact.

She might have been checking up on me. I had been out sick the last month of the previous school year —a little brain damage—all better now. I'm not supposed to do martial arts anymore, that was the main lasting effect. Avoid getting punched in the head. Also avoid lifting the heavier weights. If it makes you grunt loudly, probably wise not to lift it. A little grunt is okay.

I explained all this to her, a girl I cannot even visual except in the most abstract terms. Graceful. Tallish. Dark hair, shoulder-length, maybe a bit longer. If I inner-squint, I visualize a cafeteria lunch tray and two mylar birthday balloons. She wanted to make sure I was okay; that was the impression that I got. A kind and caring person. I appreciated this. She was someone who had started off eleventh grade with writing issues—the usual stuff, no paragraphs, run-on sentences—but over the course of the year, she took care of those problems and now was aloft, on her own, college-bound.

I must have done a good job assuring her that I was okay because I never saw her again, not even in the hallway.

*

Holding back is how it is over the long haul of the school year and also in the pedagogic moment. Even when I could go on and on about how Samuel Johnson compiled the first English dictionary by himself in a year. Samuel Johnson was so disfigured by infant scrofula that as a grown man he looked like a scarred monster and children backed away from him, one more reason why Samuel Johnson's own attempts at school teaching failed. Samuel Johnson's best friend was a convicted murderer. Samuel Johnson addressed homelessness in his neighborhood by inviting unhoused people to live with him. All of this matters urgently, but not so urgently that I keep at it for more than seven minutes. The length of "Layla" is as far as I go. After seven minutes, nothing matters more than giving students a break, so I stop.

I do not stop so they can ask questions. I stop on humanitarian grounds. When students have questions, they ask, unprompted, immediately, interrupting. One of the best ways to get an unruly class to simmer down is to ask if anyone has questions.

Nowadays, of course, online, there is no unruliness. On Zoom, the students assemble as black rectangles, hard not to imagine as stacked coffins.

I combat morbid imagery with my microphone in its flexible, expandable and retractable metal-arm mic stand: remote learning high school English teacher as DJ / public radio personality. I brush my lips against the microphone's soft foam cover. I balance my nose upon it, like a seal. Someone, somewhere, should be having fun. During COVID times, during school hours, that's me.

Enthusiasm.

Contagious.

*

Teacher love is also not father-daughter love. I know this because I became a teacher in my heart the moment my twin daughters, formerly the squirmy infants I had swaddled like burritos in my cotton T-shirts, strode down the aisle of the Castle Heights Elementary School auditorium to join their kindergarten teachers. You can't get rid of me that fast, I vowed, and soon thereafter signed up for teacher training school.

Yet father-daughter love does not equate to teacher-student love, as the most recalcitrant fifth grader in my first-ever class pointed out: "You got your daughters at home to love you, Mister. We ain't here for that."

I did talk about my daughters a lot in class until I realized, belatedly, that this alienated the students. What about us, was their perfectly understandable response. You had to put all the handprint-in-wet-cement memories aside and focus on the children in front of you.

Teacher love is also not love for all of humankind. You can't be all nice like that. Otherwise, kids naturally get distracted by thinking about how they can take advantage of you. Strict, but not mean. Never mean. This is a matter of self-preservation, as anything you do that might humiliate a student is certain to come back at you tenfold.

When I talk about how much of teaching is about holding back, I mean holding back not only many good intentions, such as solving problems for them, but also bad intentions such as sarcasm and snappy retorts of any kind. There is no coming back from raising of the voice in anger; the breakage there is permanent and light does not get in.

So teacher love is not father-daughter love, nor love of humanity, but it does consist to some degree of controlled rage. Herein lies a clue.

What is the teacher raging about? The distance between the real and the ideal.

The ideal is, we are all immersed in close reading of diverse, relevant authors; and in our own writing, matching nuanced claims with fine-tuned detail.

The real is, I have an entire class worth of kids missing because of COVID-19. What is the love that enables a remote teacher to navigate the chasm of mass absence?

*

I reached out with electronic messaging to the 60 of my 220 students who hadn't turned in any work at all by mid-semester—"I don't have any record of you turning anything in. Does that sound right? What's happening?"

Half of those sixty kids get back to me.

They say:

Both of my parents are in the hospital. I'm taking care of my three brothers.

Or,

I'm not in the best place, mentally. Even the simplest things are hard to do.

Whatever their situation, they all say this—I'll try to get some work turned in tomorrow.

The 30 kids who don't get back to me: that's an entire class worth of kids, missing. In a typical year, you'll have four or five kids ghost on you like that. I tallied these missing kids and sent the list to the attendance counselor, then turned my attention back to the students who are hanging in there.

*

One of the highest forms of teacher love is giving a kid a book. That's the exchange: not a rose or a ring. The book. I don't care if I ever get these books back. Let them do their good off the shelf, in the world. Books I have let go include *Before You Suffocate Your Own Fool Self, I am Not Your Perfect Mexican Daughter,* the graphic novel version of anything, and twice—this is vinyl, not a book—*Good Kid, m.A.A.d City.*

Yet many is the time I have had books I recommended to a kid left on the desk after class. I tell kids it's okay if they don't want to read it because I didn't write it, but this is not true. The book left on the desk is an arrow to the soul, so one way I know the soul is immortal is that I keep giving books away.

I have one kid in my English Language Development class: she really wants to reclassify so she can end being branded deficient in English and instead take a dance class. I dropped *Children of Blood and Bone* at the heavily plexi-glassed school front desk for her to pick up. I have another kid in AP English Language. She told me she's dyslexic but wanted to take the class for the challenge. For her I left *The Song of Achilles.*

Sometimes I wonder if my practice with students is really love or just common decency. For example, I always put a graphic on anything I hand out to them, or nowadays, share online. An all-text form feels too soul-sucking, like I'm making them do their taxes. The graphic may relate to the topic, or not. Armadillos are always good. Back when we were in the classroom, the graphic gave many students something to color in. I don't know what they do with them now.

I greet each one of my kids on Zoom. Howdy, how are you, how's it going. They say fine, fine, okay. If they say great, I ask, "How'd you get the upgrade?" and they say, "I just woke up in a good mood" or "My dog licked me and he doesn't usually lick me."

Licking is good. Just don't lick that dog back!

Flexibility on deadlines: love or decency? When the world is engulfed by pandemic, when the state of California has been on fire and is likely to be on fire again: is this the time to be a stickler for deadlines? I used to be a big "a deadline is a deadline, because that's the way real life works" guy but not anymore. How does real life work now?

I don't know, but these days I am much more encouraging about revisions. You can do an assignment over three times for a higher grade. Revising is learning.

Kids have a hard time believing this. They ask over and over, "Can I get a better grade if I redo it?"

The answer is always yes.

8

Climate and Classroom Change, Part 1

I want to do my part to preserve human life on earth, but what I *really* want is for my high school students to read more independently.

The students at my school are already the nicest kids in the entire Los Angeles Unified School District, recognized as such by the experts: substitute teachers who never, ever want to leave. The sheer pleasantness of our students may have something to do with the fact that our school is an arts school, where performing theater or dance or making visual art or music for part of the day seems to soothe the adolescent beast. Still, what even these talented and endearing youngsters generally will *not* do is read much outside of class.

This is due to multiple interrelated factors, mainly coming down to the fact that kids hate reading assigned books. Telling anyone they have to do anything is going to crush a lot of the joy out of it. My kids chronicled that joy-crushing process during the first week of school, when I assigned them—you bet I'm part of the problem!—to write about their development as readers and writers, using as models Richard Ford's "Reading" and Tajja Isen's "Tiny White People Took Over My Brain."

Oh, how happy reading kids once were: the joy Ivory in eighth period felt as a four-year-old, encountering a bunch of letters and realizing they spelled the word *color*. How thrilled Jason in third period felt to experience writing as superpower, akin to shooting lasers out of his eyes, simply by scrawling out his made-up adventures together with the Wimpy Kid from *Diary of a Wimpy Kid*. Yet somewhere around the middle of middle school, for most of them, the thrill was gone. "I read so many difficult and frustrating books," wrote Portia, "that I never found myself at home wanting to read for my own 'pleasure.'"

When young people put pleasure in quotes, you know they're both bright and alienated.

Still, for virtually all of my students, the memory at least of having once enjoyed reading is still there. Given that these dire times demand drastic measures, I thought we might try the mad experiment of reviving the pleasure of reading by giving students more choice about what we read this year. Not total freedom; honestly, these guys just haven't heard of enough good books to make informed choices. Instead, the experiment was to see how they respond to Lit Hub's climate change library of 365 books, along with Kim Marie Walker's addendum to that list adding more black authors and discussing the intersection of race and environmental justice.

The idea of reading about climate change came partly from wanting to do something to avert global catastrophe, but mostly from my own pettiness and petulance. At the end of last year, a few students reported on my end-of-the-year survey that they thought the class hadn't been challenging enough. *Harrumph*, said I to myself. *You want challenge? Let's read about climate change.*

Thus, in the second week of school, I introduced the topic with the podcast "It's Time to Talk about Climate Change" from KCRW's *To the Point,* hosted by the sagacious Warren Ulney. His guest was *LA Times* science writer Julia Rosen, and practically everyone in class took diligent notes as she discussed her recent story about a survey from the Yale Program on Climate Communication and the George Mason University Center for Climate Change. This survey found that although 69 percent of Americans believe climate change is real, only 37 percent talk about it "occasionally" or "often." The researchers dubbed this gap "climate silence," which is a problem because people who never talk about climate change tend to believe it is much more open to question than it actually is.

Simply talking about climate change makes people more aware of the overwhelming scientific consensus that climate change is real and man-made. This awareness, in turn, makes people more reflective on their own individual carbon footprint. As Kara said after listening to the podcast, "It makes you feel that talking about climate change could actually help."

Teen talk is an abundant and renewable natural resource. To emphasize the ways that teenagers are transforming talk about climate change into power, we also watched and discussed the trailer for an episode of The Weekly from *The New York Times* about the youth-led Sunrise Movement. The opening scene—which showed California Senator Dianne Feinstein harshing out climate-change activist elementary school kids—riled my charges up. "We're impatient," said Noemi. "We want change *now.*"

My students really want humanity to survive; I really want them to read more. We compromised by exploring the Lit Hub climate lists. When I gave the assignment—to respond in a short essay to the list in general, and recommend one or two titles—they took up the challenge.

Jacinda wondered, "How is it that for all these years, when we have had such books and authors who were well aware of climate change, do we just start to face it now?" We talked about the history of oil companies who suppressed the findings of scientists they hired to explore the risks of auto emissions. I dreamt of Jacinda reading Daniel Yergin's epic on the oil industry, *The Prize*, and just a few weeks later, she borrowed it.

There is also sadness. That's what Casandra reported feeling when she read the Lit Hub list: "Just reading a simple summary about each book made me sad. They touched me in a way that made me regret doing anything to ever hurt the planet." It's good to have tenderness in the mix, along with the usual and still-important stuff about comprehension and grammar. Tenderness and sadness and regret and caring:

those are some things that might inspire more reading outside of class. I'm so curious now to see how Casandra applies this tenderness to our reading in class.

So, what should that reading be? My students have spoken. I tallied every single title they said they'd want to read, and the outcome is incontestable. They want to read two titles in particular, and in general, everything else.

Their number one request is... *The Jungle.* Name-recognition played a big role here (of the title, not the author—one kid dubbed him "Uptown" Sinclair). Kids have heard about *The Jungle* in history classes; they know it's responsible for getting consumer protection legislation passed over 100 years ago. Already this means they know more about *The Jungle* than almost any other book without wizards. Teaching experts tell us: start with what they know!

"It talks about how human rights and animal rights are similar," wrote Hannah, who is curious to learn about how violation of those rights leads to "damaging our planet." I'm curious to see how the kids at our Title 1 (read, high poverty) school respond to Upton Sinclair's depiction of working in a slaughterhouse and living in a tenement. It's my kids' parents who tend to work two or three jobs, and their families who get priced out when neighborhoods gentrify.

I also have a personal goal for *The Jungle.* The last time I tried to read it with a class, I bailed when the family breadwinner, man-mountain turned slaughterhouse worker Jurgis, thus far impervious to the hellish conditions, finally hurts his leg on the job. Even though I myself read *The Jungle* in high school, I couldn't bear to recall the consequences of his workplace injury. This time—with my students' support—I hope to become a more courageous reader.

The second book they asked to read, or re-read, is *The Lorax.* Wanting to read the easiest thing possible played a big role here, but not the only role. Students really do like to use what they know, and they know *The Lorax* is a parable of climate change. "*The Lorax* also shows a very real important factor to climate change which is that humans are filled with greed," wrote Yessenia. Students were eager to talk about the connection between human psychology and the environment, and I look forward to continuing that conversation. I really wish that even one of them had made the connection between the clear-cutting of the Truffula trees in *The Lorax* to the burning of the Amazon rainforest, but no one did. It makes you wonder what they actually know, and what they need to learn, which fortunately is exactly what a teacher should be wondering at the start of the school year.

Connecting with the Dr. Seuss-loving little kids who still live inside these charismatic almost-adults is powerful pedagogy. So I will gladly read *The Lorax* out loud and also show them the pictures. They're ready for a more sophisticated response. "I find the patterns and rhythmic writing to be super cool and unique," Kadence wrote. "They remind me of when I was a kid and they bring back fun and exciting, yet also some sad memories. I find that enduring, to remember the past but in a sense of letting it go." She knows that in reading about climate change, we will be doing a lot of remembering the environmental past. And letting it go.

As Eleanor put it, "Many of the books seemed to be about the glory in nature we will soon be missing." Eleanor is an especially bright kid who doesn't especially want to read either *The Lorax* or *The Jungle*. She is intrigued by what the Lit Hub list called the "wild and saintly" voice of Annie Dillard. She'd also like to explore *The Lost Daughter* by Mary Williams, who she trusts must have a lot to say as the daughter of a Black Panther who was raised by Jane Fonda and hiked the Appalachian Trail. This leads us to the third most popular book from the lists: all of them.

The 28 kids in Period 8, for example, recommended a total of 35 different titles. Those kids want to read *On the Origin of Species, Under the Sea Wind, The Cooking Gene, Animal Liberation* and 31 other books. To me, this suggests a nascent literary diversity, a healthy change from the monotony of reading the same overly familiar books over and over and over again, often from one grade to another. *To Kill a Mockingbird, The Great Gatsby, Romeo and Juliet, 1984:* they really are all great. I love and have taught them all. And: the forced reading of these and other perennial titles reminds me a lot, in the context of climate change, of factory-farming; in particular, it reminds me of Michael Pollan's revolting descriptions of force-feeding corn to cows in *The Omnivore's Dilemma.* Today's teens need creativity as a matter of survival in addressing climate change. That creativity will not prosper with a strict literary diet of the same old, same old.

The question I'm left with is, how are we actually going to read all of these books about climate change? To get us started, I have bought a ton of these books for the classroom. Extravagant spending on classroom supplies is simply what teachers do. But me just buying all the books is not sustainable, and given my newly awakened consciousness around consumption, I might have to rethink my book-buying habit. Now *that* is what I call an inconvenient truth. It may turn out that teaching my students to become more independent readers will involve motivating them to get their own books. It would certainly be a hopeful sign.

Meanwhile, DonorsChoose will, blessedly, get us some classroom sets, and there are lots of grants out there for classroom libraries. The even bigger challenge, as it is so often with books, is not getting them, but reading and discussing and acting on them. Coordinating all of this diverse reading on climate change into academic progress—having the students actually learn what they need to know—that's the biggest challenge. Which is, after all, what we wanted. Let's go!

9

Climate and Classroom Change, Part 2

They started reading in book groups, assiduously.

At first. They're always assiduous the first day of book groups. If you ever want to see the universe tending towards entropy, check out an in-class book group by Day Three.

Kids say they can't read because they don't have the book when the books are neatly piled near the milkweed plant. Kids have the book but instead of discussing how the way the slaughterhouse treats animals is like the way humans treat the earth, they instead argue over what is the worst Beastie Boys song, or whether the last syllable of the word l-a-v-e-n-d-e-r is pronounced "ur" or "are."

This is high school.

Nevertheless, about half the kids are indeed reading or discussing a climate change-related book, mostly *The Jungle* but also *Sand County Almanac, Ill Nature, A Negro Explorer at the North Pole,* and both Asian and Latin American folktales. Overall, my students are as focused as any grown-up book club I have ever experienced. Yes, I want more from the seemingly off-topic kids, but you can't force it. This latitude enables them to reach Day Four, when they were back to reading so assiduously you could hear a pin drop. I dropped a pin, to make sure. It sounded like this: click, softer click, almost inaudible click.

Whether they are independently reading or independently not-reading, what I want now is for them to ask their own questions, research them, and use their findings to generate new questions. This is not how it's usually done in school. Usually, you read the assigned text, then answer the questions at the back, and that's it: question, answer, done. This provides a semblance of order at the price of killing creativity, which seemed fine until we broke the planet. Now The Answer—eliminate carbon pollution—is all but written by a bloody finger in the sky. That's why I think it would be good for my students to pursue their own authentic questions in response to the imperative of reinventing how we live.

Thus, while I was all for us reading *The Lorax,* we paired it with Alan Weisman's survey in *The New York Review of Books* of *The Uninhabitable Earth* and the latest manifesto from Bill McKibben. Take a kindergarten book, pair it with the *NYRB* and it averages out right about at high school level.

Their questions about these texts fall into three main categories: scientific, economic, and political. The scientific questions tend to start out adorable and end up horrible. For example, the story of The Lorax is told by a failed industrialist named the Once-ler, who is living as a hermit in the ruined landscape of his former factories. He charges a fee to tell his tale, and the fee includes the whimsical "shell of a great great great grandfather snail."

This got Harmoni wondering "if a snail could even live long enough to become a great great great grandfather." She looked it up online and discovered that, in her words, "a snail can live to see a whopping 52 generations." The bleak prospects laid out in Weisman's gloss on *The Uninhabitable Earth* caused Harmoni to wonder further, "If a snail born today will live to see their 52nd great grandchildren, would a human born today have a chance to see their own children before our world becomes uninhabitable?"

That's one way to defuse the climate bomb: turn it into a parody of a math test word problem. Technically, this doesn't remove carbon dioxide from the atmosphere, but it's funny. Funny reduces fear and fends off hopelessness.

Many students feel emboldened, at this point, to question the economics of climate change. Zipporah asked, "Why is money deemed more powerful than the environment?"

"Why" questions are notoriously hard to answer, but Zipporah was totally down to borrow Naomi Klein's *This Changes Everything: Capitalism vs. the Climate.* I had splurged for a teetering pile of climate economics books as soon as I read her question, fantasizing that even though I am whelmed with grading papers, my homework/rehearsal/college applications/being teenagers-whelmed students would read all the books I wish I could read.

Zipporah, for example, is a bright, good-natured kid. It is my fond hope that by honing in on some Naomi Klein, she will figure out a way to combine what is best in human nature with what is fair and just in economics, and tell the world, and the world listen and act, so that instead of a mere book report the result of her reading will be a global picnic with the theme, "Whew, That Was a Close One!" featuring a tug-of-war, three-legged race, and proper commemoration of all we have already irreparably lost.

Yes, I have high expectations of my students. Should the results of Zipporah's reading prove less than messianic, I'm confident she'll learn some good SAT words and gain useful background knowledge to bring to the written portion of the AP English Lang exam. Something good will come of this climate study, even if my 150 students are not collectively responsible for saving the world like a hero snipping the yellow wire on the infinity bomb with .01 seconds to go on the timer. Climate change doesn't even work like a bomb, and we aren't going to save the world all at once. It will happen one question at a time.

Portia questions the utter ineffectiveness of The Lorax, a woodland sprite who claims to speak for the trees clear-cut by the Once-ler. Speak he may, but the Lorax does nothing to stop deforestation other than tell the Once-ler that he's destroying habitat. "Why was it all just preach?" Portia asked. "Why was the Lorax all talk, no action?"

These teenagers know this is their time. Elias gave a call to action while dismissing the glimmer of hope offered at the end of *The Lorax*. He says it's just a silly sliver of Seuss, whose whimsy can't save the real world. Because of a lack of a rambunctious rhymer as humanity's author, Elias concluded, the time has come for young people to be their own authors.

That's where we're going from here. Specifically, we're going on literary road trips in a collective quest for climate-related questions, answers, and further questions. Eleventh graders will head north on the 101, driving straight into Marc Reisner's *Cadillac Desert,* which questions what people are even doing living in the Southwest. Good thing teens love existential dread! We'll pack those lessons into the Sierras with John Muir, then go to Oakland to hang with Native American youth in Tommy Orange's *There, There*. "The land is everywhere or nowhere," Tommy Orange says. What does that mean? We'll make our best guesses and learn what we can.

In both classes, we'll make the literary voyage home, to tell our tale. How to tell it: that's another question for this journey. I do know that along with existential dread, these art school teens love set design. The time has come for us to be our own authors; we can be actors, too.

10

Reading Gain in the Era of Learning Loss

My 11th and 12th graders did not do "learning loss." Instead, according to our district-mandated reading assessment, we started in August 2020 at an average LEXILE-based reading level of 10.0 and finished in June 2021 at level 12.4.

I asked my students what they thought accounted for this trend-bucking improvement, and they basically said: shrug.

Students don't really like it when you ask them about teaching. That's your job, they are too polite to come right out and say. But I do think someone should say something about how we managed to defy the odds, so let me share what I think is replicable and scalable about our success.

1. Assign this for homework: Ask your students to explain why four to seven interesting and not already completely familiar words make sense in their independent reading. For structure, give them a spreadsheet with one column for the word, another for the sentence and citation, a third for their explanation of the word's meaning in context. The fourth column is the payoff: Why does it make sense for the author to use that word in this sentence?

This encourages students to think about a text as a thing that has been created, with meaning they can discover and interpret for themselves. Furthermore, public school students are willing to do vocabulary homework. It feels right to them. So be it.

Don't insist that they use the spreadsheet. It's just a model. The key here is letting them discover their own words and meanings. Three sample words that pop up from a random student's work: manifold, synthesis, province. Students develop reading power when they grasp the meaning of such evocative vocabulary for themselves.

2. Encourage almost complete reading independence. We would typically read an anchor text together, such as the short story "Gryphon" by Charles Baxter, about a bizarre substitute teacher or the essay "Until Black Women are Free, None of Us Will Be Free" by Keeanga-Yamahtta Taylor.

This would get us started on exploring such questions as "What is education?" and "What is freedom?" To continue the exploration, I encouraged students to choose from titles ranging from "American Conservatism: Reclaiming An Intellectual Tradition" to "The Combahee River Collective Statement." They didn't have to read the whole thing, just enough to have something to think and write about.

I also gave students the freedom to pick one book they wanted to read to go with one book from my long list of recommendations. My main restrictions were that I did not want to hear about these three titles: "Go Ask Alice," "The Outsiders" and "A Child Called It."

I find these books symptomatic of raging generational illiteracy, and it makes me crazy whenever they are the only book a student can summon. I didn't tell them that, however, because no one likes a party pooper. I simply reminded the students about keeping the audience in mind and told them that as the main audience for their writing, I simply had heard enough about these books.

This explanation must have sufficed because no one decided they needed to practice their own remix version of antidisestablishmentarianism by reading one of those please-don't titles.

We did exchange some texts about books it would or wouldn't be OK for them to read, and I did sigh whenever it was something they had obviously already read and had picked just to get it over with. But whatever they wanted to read on their own was almost always OK because I would willingly, if not happily, trade literary merit for student autonomy.

4. Let students know the results of their reading tests. I have yet to come across a student who does not want to read at or above grade level. However, they can't act upon that desire if they don't know where they stand. So each of the three times we took the district-mandated test, I went to some trouble to share the report from the testing company about what the student's next steps could be. I don't know why they can't access this information themselves, but as I often say when facing gigantic educational bureaucracies, oh well.

I would like to say I then differentiated instruction for each student according to their needs; however, we haven't come all this way for me to start lying to you now. There were some students who were so heartbreakingly low, I did make some accommodations for them in terms of sharing books like "The Poet X" and "brown girl dreaming" and "The Crossover." I feel a moral obligation to reach out that way to high school kids reading at elementary school levels.

Everybody else, I pretty much let them self-differentiate by choosing their own reading and vocabulary. I also gave them choices of topics to write about.

For example, you could write about whether you agreed that until Black women are free, none of us will be free; or, if that was not the topic for you, that's OK because *The New York Times* has 300 other things you can argue about; and if you don't like any of those, then you might further consider the vast array of topics on Allsides, a supposedly unbiased but I think really pretty conservative site. And that's ok. Someone's gotta be conservative. Otherwise, we would all be thinking alike and that is not the way it is.

The point is that students can make impressive gains in reading even under severely suboptimal circumstances if guided and encouraged to think for themselves.

MARK GOZONSKY

11

How to Teach the Russian Invasion of Ukraine

The first step in teaching the Russian invasion of Ukraine is noticing that your students need to talk about it. I realized this during 4th period on Thursday, February 24, 2022. My 10th graders were more glum than usual. They're usually very glum, due to being 15 years old and their transition between middle and high school having been ruined by COVID. They express this glumness by frowning and sighing and not turning in any work. Thursday's glumness was characterized by even more frowning and sighing, as well as something new, a look of suppressed panic, as if many kids were about to scream.

What's all this about, I wondered, until an exceptionally cordial student asked me, "So what's your opinion about World War III?"

That's how I realized that my students needed to talk about the Russian invasion of Ukraine. As a result, I took the following steps the next day, with positive results.

1. **Find an informative article for students to read in class.** My students hearkened to a *NY Times* explainer. An especially bright kid said when we talked about it, "It's nice to read something unbiased." I asked them to take between five and ten notes, in order to be ready for the next step.

2. **Have students discuss the article among themselves.** We use the Partner A- Partner B protocol, which basically means talking to the person across from you. I almost always have students talk to each other before I get involved. They tend to learn and remember from peer interaction, and these conversations also let them rehearse before speaking to the entire class. You can meanwhile circulate, gauging the interest level while semi-unobtrusively eavesdropping to find out who might have something especially worthwhile to share. The interest level on the Russian invasion of Ukraine was high. Everybody talking, leaning in – not frowning!

3. **Hold a Community Circle.** You could just call on kids in their seats, but for a topic this important, it's worth telling them to move their seats into a circle or at least a blob where no one has their back to anyone and everyone can see everyone else's face. When the topic is something people have strong feelings about, it's good to see everyone's faces, or at least their eyes above their masks. There is an entire protocol for conducting a community circle, the gist of which is to speak and listen from the heart; don't worry about what you're going to say, just say it; and say just enough to make your point. You also have the right to pass. That is an entire community circle workshop in one paragraph!

My students' remarks on the Russian invasion of Ukraine fit into five categories: empathy for the people of Ukraine, fear of World War III, criticism of Putin, criticism of memes that treat the invasion as a joke, and geopolitical curiosity.

We haven't gotten to understatement yet, but here's how one student expressed empathy: "It's kind of unfortunate to wake up to a bomb exploding." Another reflected on "How scared they must be." A third observed, "They're looking for shelter in – what do you call them?"

A classmate suggested, "Bunkers." She agreed: "Yah, bunkers."

The students' fear of World War III shows they're paying attention in their history classes: "The United States has said before that it wasn't going to get involved in a European ground war."

Another student wondered: "The U.S. troops in Poland. How will that turn out?"

A third said, "If the Russians send a nuke, the U.S. won't retaliate because that would cause nuclear winter.

These dire remarks showed a much keener grasp of history than I would have thought these guys had in them. I am jaded from years of students not knowing the dates of the Civil War. They may not have been paying attention before, but they're definitely paying attention now.

They are critical of Putin, especially for refusing to take Ukraine president Zelinsky's phone call stating that the people of Ukraine want peace. Putin, they say, is vain, threatened, humiliated, "an overbearing parent." A student in my other class of 10th-graders said she thought Putin was remorseful, and this set off a big discussion of how he is anything but remorseful. That student came up to me after class to say the word she meant was resentful.

My students expressed geopolitical curiosity: "How can wars be fought economically?" A student wondered about the ramifications of world leaders conducting foreign policy on social media. Another wondered why war is still happening today.

I didn't try to answer. My job is to nod understandingly when people have had their say, and to look encouragingly at whoever wants to go next. Students agreed that memes making a joke of the situation were inappropriate, but also a means of coping. "People outside of Ukraine are the ones making memes," said the girl who had noted how unpleasant it is to wake up to bombing. "Ukraine teens aren't joking."

In the midst of our discussion in 7th period, I heard a boy say, "Existential dread." That was it. There it was. We got our feelings out and as a result, felt better. I know this because I asked, after we finished talking about Ukraine, how did it feel – in just a few words – to do the community circle. "Good," most people said, with no one passing.

"Good."

"Good."

"Not bad."

Even the glummest kid of all, the one who has refused to do any work all year, who sits with his arms crossed, who told me the reason he doesn't turn in any work is because he doesn't feel like it and he doesn't know or care what the consequences will be – even that kid, going around the circle, describing how it felt to talk about the Russian invasion of Ukraine together as a class, even that kid said it was good.

In My Backyard

12

The Third Example

It began with wanting another seed starter kit, because the first seed starter kit had re-enacted the dawn of creation, and after it was full, my wife asked if I could please also plant dill.

A seed starter kit consists of two black plastic trays and a clear plastic dome. The first tray is like a big black ice cube tray with spaces for 50 cubes of growing medium, a spongy combination of fine-ground sphagnum moss, compost, and soil. Push bigger seeds into a pencil-tip sized hole. Leave tiny seeds on the surface. Place the first tray into the second tray. Add water. Cover with dome. Marvel at the origins of life.

Condensation will soon occur. The dome has two vents at the top, so you can manage the level of humidity. You create your own weather, like a classroom teacher, according to the inevitable quote in any professional development about classroom management -- except that in a seed starter kit, the weather is always good. Seedlings soon sprout and you see them in their very first springing. The first emergence of root, the first upthrusting of stem, the first unfurling of leaf. It is good.

Many people use their seed starter kits to cultivate marijuana, but I prefer not to. In my first kit I started amaranth, cucumber, feverfew, Vulcan lettuce, jalapeño and Italian Marconi Golden pepper, primrose, acorn squash, and green zebra tomato. I bought that kit online but could not wait to get the second one, because when my wife asked me to plant dill to go with the cucumber, I wanted to accommodate her immediately.

It occurred to me that there is a hydroponics warehouse two blocks away from our house, which is in a West LA neighborhood that used to be fields of lima beans. Surely they would have a seed starter kit. Indeed they did, and so much more: vast plumbing infrastructures, giant fans as well as giant fan silencers, so many grow lamps, and a bazaar of bottled fertilizers. The fertilizers especially appealed to my teacherly yearning to cultivate transformational growth. Seed starter kit number one had come with its own dainty little fertilizer, the size of a hotel room shampoo bottle. The fertilizers at the hydroponics store promised such superior fecundity, I needed to get one and experiment.

The clerk inquired as to what I would be growing, in blatant contradiction of a big sign by the cash register proclaiming, "Grow whatever you want, but don't tell us or we'll be required by law to ask you to leave." Surrounded by so much industrial weed growing equipment, I felt guilty by association, but managed to stammer that I'd be growing peppers, cucumbers and various garden herbs.

"Various garden herbs," he confirmed, and escorted me back to the fertilizer aisle. The entire store was immaculate. It made silicon chip manufacturing plants look like the shaggiest of Telegraph Avenue second-hand clothing stores. My clerk, who wore his septum piercing with aplomb, proceeded to compare and contrast the offerings with the assurance of a veteran stockbroker recommending a prudent yet aggressive portfolio.

Since as much as I love my seedlings, I will not be sending any of them to college, I asked him to recommend the one fertilizer he most highly recommended. He considered this gravely, then forthrightly held out this thick soft plastic bottle which now stands before me. It does not visibly throb, nor does it bubble one big bubble every minute on the minute, as if containing a small drakken, punctually biding its time.

The bottle is motionless. I am the one quivering with foreboding of the effects that one and half teaspoons of its sepia murk will have on the carrots and all other life forms in my backyard. RootRock – for that is the name of this plant elixir -- is supposedly distilled from sugar beets, according to the scant information available online, yet it smells distinctly like fermented undergarments.

I do not recall the precise moment when it dawned on me that I could use RootRock in the garden just as readily as a supplement for the second seed starter kit. Who was going to stop me? This is a question that often comes up in adulthood, and when the answer is "no one," as it so often is, then you're on your own.

I poured the stuff out surreptitiously in one of my wife's kitchen measuring spoon—yes, I admit to that. I admit to it all. I mixed it with tap water in a 2-liter Coke bottle of much thinner plastic than the nuclear reactor grade plastic containing the RootRock. Oh, how that Coke bottle darkened, as though what amounted to no more than several big drops of RootRock had turned day to night, yang to yin, and one further example, the third and most dreadful, of something light becoming dark.

Yet even as I beheld the concoction, I knew that I would not hesitate to carry out my plan to fertilize the carrots, or rather, not hesitate any further, even though it would have been nice to think of a third example. Let it be, I told myself. The third example will come in time. And so I ventured out of the kitchen into the backyard.

I had pre-watered the carrots because everybody knows you have to water your vegetables before you fertilize or you will chemical-burn the roots. That would be bad! I had noticed when soaking the carrots that one plant actually was carroting up very nicely. It was crowning. I was really glad to see this because all of my previous carrot ventures have been flops. It hurts to write this, but it's true, and apparently it's true what they say about the truth setting you free, because already the shame is transforming into strength. I can feel it.

The truth is, I fertilized the carrots even though they didn't need fertilizing. They were doing fine as natural carrots, but I wanted to see what would happen, and I still do. I want to see if RootRock turns natural carrot into John the Conqueror root, or perhaps an entirely different kind of root that's never been pulled from the ground and cannot in fact be pulled out by anyone but me. I am not afraid anymore. Just the opposite.

I am the third example.

Wow. That stuff really is strong.

13

House of Straw

I am easily outwitted by chickens. For example, all four of my young hens can easily fly the coop –a valuable lesson, the phrase itself, so literally true. Here I have spent my entirely urban lifetime thinking "fly the coop" means to escape; now I know it means you can devote hours and hours to fencing in your hens with chicken wire, mesh, siding, more chicken wire and more mesh – and still your hens get out and either cluck, cluck, cluck all over your garden or else stay right outside the perimeter you have tried and failed to reinforce, looking at you as though you are your mirror image, not really there.

For these four golden-brown-browner-brownest hens, it's either pecking, nesting, clucking, ruffling, fluttering, roosting, brooding, pooping -- or nothing. It is not blankness or stupidity you see in a chicken's eye. It is single-minded focus, which I patently lack and which currently gives them the edge when it comes to outwitting me.

Yet every day I get closer to being smarter. I have come to understand, for example, that to be "chicken" as in afraid does not refer to a chicken's lack of courage. It means being afraid to fight a chicken, who is formidable in her own very specific and resolute way. I learned this from my dog Chip, who sometimes helps me get them back in the coop at night by barking, at which he is a true champ. He will also occasionally flush them out of a bush, for which he gets to sleep on a pillow in me and my wife's bedroom after years of being banished to the garage. He deserves this major upgrade because he is now a working dog, even though he also sometimes flat out runs away, overwhelmed by the fluttering of these squat, beaked, feathered beasts.

In these precious moment when my little doggie shows exactly what it means to be chicken, I feel enveloped by a beam of etymological insight, like when a knight is traversing a forest and a single ray of light bursts through the treetops to illuminate the true meaning of gallantry. And just as Sir Gawain shall never turn away from the challenge of the Green Knight, neither will I back down from this battle of wits with chickens. On the contrary, I am just getting started.

My favorite of all chicken barriers is mesh: seemingly infinite folds of black plastic webbing that sticks to things you yourself didn't even register as being there, like the buttons on the cuff of the long-sleeve shirt you are wisely wearing while gardening. The sheer stickiness of mesh has led or misled me to feel undue confidence in mesh as barrier, for though it is sticky, it is also fantastically fragile, held in place by sticks and twigs.

Sometimes I merely shove the mesh deep into a bush, on the logic that if I have trouble extricating myself when a button gets caught, think of how the mesh will stick to all the nubbins and twiglets within the bush; or, according to internet --:--:-- - }} >> = = = nodes, internodes, lateral buds and bundle scars. Even here amid phase one of the climate apocalypse, there is still so much to know and learn and feel.

I imagine chickens on the inside and potential predators on the outside tangling with the web of mesh, getting caught, getting frustrated, giving up. I also think A LOT about the Three Little Pigs and how right now I am definitely at House of Straw level. Start where they're at, that's the teacher's credo, and I'm a teacher, so it's a physician-heal-thyself situation. I would build a brick henhouse if I could, but I only have six bricks, which I try using to prop up the water bowl the chickens continue to topple.

Frankly, I wouldn't mind the hens free-ranging if wild animals weren't so audacious nowadays. This is why I feel compelled to protect the hens from their own curious and free-ranging natures. Due to hardly anybody driving anymore, wild animals don't have to worry as much about getting run over. Also, the air is cleaner, giving creatures greater lung capacity and stamina. And, of course, they can smell human fear. For example, Timothy the Squirrel darts in and out of our kitchen, nabbing cat food. That's unsettling. It would be a sign of the apocalypse were the apocalypse not already upon us.

To me, all squirrels are named Timothy, one among many instances of animal prejudice I need to reckon with as part of an overall realignment of myself and nature. It can't be Me versus Nature anymore. Human arrogance in general has got to go. This was obvious in the before-times and now is being trumpeted with every birdsong in the birdsong-intensive soundscape and lofted with every puffy-then-wispy-then-puffy-again cloud in the bluer-than-ever sky.

Step One of rectifying my prejudice and discrimination against nature could indeed be allowing Lucky, Clucky, Plucky and Kentucky free range. I would do that if I didn't feel sure that a hawk will dive straight down out of that bluer-than-ever sky and carry one or more of my emotional support chickens away. I could do without their eggs – they haven't even laid any eggs yet, that's how young they are – but I would be hard-pressed to replace the emotional support I get from having something to protect, however feebly.

I'm invested in these particular feathered friends. Plucky – always the first or last one out, brown-feathered, her comb orange soda diluted by melted ice. Lucky – exactly like Plucky but not so willing to stick her neck out with its redder, more fresh-on-the-vine strawberry comb. Clucky is resplendent in her gold and brown collar and Kentucky is pure gold and of all these plump poultry, the plumpest.

We've been in this thing together ever since I let them out of the cardboard box I got from a guy in Westminster two days before lockdown and built them their own coop from a kit I bought at PetCo from the very first person I met with knuckles bleeding from washing her hands so often. My own handiwork in constructing the coop impressed my wife, so that was a plus, but between you and me, this coop is *f-l-i-m-s-y*. Do not even touch it with more than one finger at a time. It is made of what appears to be cedar-color painted balsa wood. If foxes make a comeback in this part of the world – on the west side of Los Angeles -- near, now that you mention it, what used to be called the Fox Hills Mall...

I hear my heart pounding. I really don't want to experience fox-in-henhouse carnage. I really want to pray, Dear God, please don't let foxes or any other emboldened critters eat my chickens and leave unwrapped capillaries and drifting dander left over to show me what's what. Let me harvest their eggs for four years and then when they're done with a privileged lifetime I'll make BBQ and chicken soup out of them, I promise.

This is further discrimination, of course: why should I be the one who gets to eat my chickens and not a fox or raccoon or hawk? I really don't have a convincing answer. I am philosophically as well as slapstick outwitted, chasing Plucky around a bush.

A solution might be just to let them free. I keep coming around to this, I know, but this time it might stick. I am writing a few days later, after realizing that I have been feeding my chickens dog food for two days. Long story. Big picture of a chicken on the bag. I have other excuses, none of them exculpatory. Let's just stipulate that two days ago I noticed they didn't like the little pellets and then yesterday, I noticed "Chicken is the main ingredient" in tiny little type on the bag. I gagged a little, then rustled up some corn meal from the freezer and some kasha from the back of the cupboard. They set to pecking right away inside their coop. Happy! Hooray! I headed off to dinner with my wife, ready to beer and ice cream my worries away, after which just this one little sub-worry still lingered: "What if buckwheat causes chickens to puff up until they explode?"

This was the irruption of long-suppressed dread first encountered in middle school, where boys in South Texas talked to each other avidly of feeding Alka-Seltzer to pelicans on the Gulf Coast so they could watch them explode. I expected to wake up this morning with exploded hen carcasses strewn about my backyard, and it wouldn't be because of a fox, it would be because of me. Before I could bear to look, I looked up "Can chickens eat buckwheat?" on the internet and the answer is --:--:-- - }} >> = = = you bet!

They can also eat clover and rye and pretty much any cover crop, which is still 90 percent of what I've got growing back here. Furthermore, they will clamber over compost, aerating and fertilizing as they go. I found all this out in an article on *Mother Earth News*, credit where it's due. This article changes everything. I'm going to re-arrange my chicken fortification today so that they can be free.

And now, writing one more day of living later, that's exactly what I did! The hens can range garden-wide, so long as I am out there with them. I really do not envision a hawk swooping down while I am planting grapes or transplanting pumpkins. That would be bold indeed. That would be a sign of a nature I am not prepared to encounter. I am prepared to encounter the hens pecking away, pooping away, keeping things fertilized and in balance, eventually laying eggs and it all being good, at which point maybe I will be able to confront the nature I am not yet prepared to encounter.

14

Epsom Salts (from "The Mushroom Farmer")

The chayote plants had arrived in such uncommonly vibrant good health that it made the mf feel extra sad when they all immediately shriveled up and died.

Oh, they were dead all right. Leaves that had arrived emphatically green, and as fully upright as all of us who are reaching for the sky — every single one of those lush leaves on each of six lovingly packed-for-shipping plants, each one representing the entirely do-able promise of a soon-forthcoming gourd paradise — they all overnight turned shit brown and as sunken down as a typically cheerful person in the depth of clinical depression.

The mf gazed upon the fallen vines and thought, dang. He thought, shucks. He was putting on a downhome front, which you have to do as a gardener if you are not going to water your garden with tears.

Inside, the mf felt disappointed but also curious. Why would such healthy plants up and die so soon? It was something to ponder.

He wanted to grow chayote because you see them in Latin produce markets *todo el tiempo*. He liked the pale green gnarliness of chayote fruit. He liked that chayote is a staple of both Central American as well as many Asian cuisines. He loved that chayote fruit have almost the exact heft of a hardball.

The mf had also seen chayote flourishing in a long-gone community garden south of downtown that had notoriously been bulldozed to make way for nothing. However, it later turned out that the city block where chayote and nopales and many beans and corns besides had flourished had, like the entire surrounding neighborhood, for decades been horrifically lead-contaminated by a nearby battery factory.

The demise of that community garden and its subsequent finding to have been a garden of poison is a sadness the mf carries with him in his heart-shaped collection of sad things with no answers.

A farmer can't be afraid to kill plants. That's a saying the mf often turns to after confronting garden sadness. Also, the mf is trying not to take things personally nowadays. He saw an ad on the internet that said, "Learn how not to take things personally." It made him think, "What if instead of clicking, I just don't take things personally from now on?"

This is a work in progress. Meanwhile, the mf felt chagrin, sprinkled with hope that the sturdy chayote seed would generate more robust vines. Hope is nice. But days passed and the withered plants degenerated further, sinking into the ground like the Wicked Witch of the West after being doused with water. They cursed him with their dying sputter, "Look at us suffer and die, we who arrived in your care at the pinnacle of health."

It had been the pinnacle, all right. The mf wrote a note to the vendor who had so meticulously wrapped the formerly happy chayote plants in paper with two bamboo spikes to protect the upright leaves from being jostled in transit and then added an additional layer of heavy-duty bubble wrap.

The mf had felt such admiration for the vendor's care in shipping the chayote vines that he wrote a note to him saying this: "I am not blaming you for their failure. I am just wondering if you had any idea what might have caused it."

The vendor wrote back, "I've never seen anything like that."

And that was it. No, "I'm so sorry the plants died." No, "Try X next time; here's a great offer on some replacement plants." No nothing.

Oh well. The mf has a theory now. The chayote plants died from shock.

That would explain the suddenness.

Maybe he should have let them acclimate to being in Southern California for a couple of days before planting them in the warm and happening dirt of his little farm. When I say "warm and happening," I mean, if you stick a hand trowel into a row of the mf's garden, it comes back up with dirt that is practically pulsing with energy, like a tiny supernova.

The chayote might have OD'd on soil. Maybe.

But maybe it was the epsom salts in particular. The mf had sprinkled epsom salts all along each row, having read back when he was making bath bombs with Mrs. mf that epsom salts can be used to encourage sprouting. "What's this now?" the mf had made a mental note by chiseling it into the soft material of his brain that might someday be repurposed as mushroom substrate.

The making of bath bombs with Mrs. mf had been a moment of splendor. "It's like something newlyweds would do," he heard Mrs. mf breathe to one of her long-time besties. Ooo-ooo-ooo, thought the mf, in spotlight letters on the marquee of his mind. I did something right!

He had been thinking they could amortize the big ol' lavender bush smack dab in the middle of the little farm by making lavender oil and using the lavender oil in bath bombs, which are little golf ball-sized agglomerations of citric acid, epsom salts, and essential oils. They go through them like crazy in the mf household on account of their aches from being on the go so much.

I mention the glory of love, as seen here in the long-married mf and Mrs. mf making bath bombs together even though the lavender oil came out stinky, something went wrong, you just have to pour that concoction down the sink right away and chalk it up to something, live and learn or live and live, they're both viable approaches, the main thing being whew, that lavender oil did not come out the way it was supposed to, oh well.

And yeah, it checks out that epsom salts sprinkled directly onto soil does what sowing salt directly into soil has historically done: kill everything. The mf has inadvertently taken out vengeance upon himself, with the chayote plants as his proxies.

It's sobering.

And yet, as it states clearly in the disco-era hit "Funky Town," you gotta move on.

By now the epsom salts have probably dissolved. The mf refuses to believe that he has permanently poisoned his own garden. It is theoretically possible and people do fork themselves over with equal or greater malfeasance day in and day out, but the mf has never considered himself to be a permanent life-fucker-upper, to speak plainly. Temporary life fucker-upper, oh sure, but permanent? Even if it's true, the mf would rather leave that like unclaimed baggage going around and around on the baggage claim carousel.

So in the spirit of I can't go on, I'll go on, the mf looked up chayote propagation and discovered you can plant the fruit directly in the ground. Huh. Who knew? Typically you are not supposed to plant grocery store vegetables, such as potatoes, directly in the ground; however, the reasons for this seem vague. Grocery store veggies are bred for consumption, not propagation. What's the diff though, you could ask. Will it trigger Armageddon to plant a supermarket yam?

So he bought two chayote from a Latin market on his bike ride home from school. These were two old, gnarly-looking chayotes, with vines starting to grow from the crown of the fruit. The lady at the market wagged a finger at the mf for picking those two, but he told her, *"Esta bien, yo quiero crecerlos y ellos ya tienan las vinas."*

This made sense to her, so she rang him up. The mf felt proud of his conversational Spanish, which determined that she had lived in the neighborhood for 20 years and that while she herself was fine, the neighborhood wasn't great. The liquor store across the street generated *muchas problemas*. Together, the mf and the grocer agreed that *alcohol es muy peligrosa.*

Then he rode his bike home and planted those two chayotes because it is still his dream to grown a great many of them and put them out on a little table in front of his house so passersby can come by and help themselves.

**The Mushroom Farmer Newsletter
Volume 2, Number 1 – July 2, 2021**

HOWDY NEIGHBOR!

I want to share a representative sample of what's growing in the backyard.

Please help yourself. Everything out here is free. I am sharing it because sharing = caring in general, and in particular, because when I look around at all these encampments, I think, "Wow, what can be done?"

FEATURE FOOD:

Come-as-You-Are Onions ft. feverfew & late nigella blossoms and seriously so much fennel

These are thrice-washed but not completely scrubbed onions, from a Short Day Sampler pack I got from Dixondale Farms back in February. The "Short Day" part has to do with what kind of onions are good to grow at what time of year – these grew from late winter 'til... today!

The yellow ones are 1015Y Texas Super Sweet, a name I like because of the very official agricultural number, and Texas and super and sweet. The white ones are Texas Early White (more Texas!). And the red ones are Red Creole onions, so all very Juneteenth-y names.

The bunching onions – well, they just volunteered. I like the enthusiasm!

I left a little patina of soil on 'em to keep it real; same with the roots.

The feverfew blossoms sure do look like chamomile, don't they? One way you can tell they're feverfew is, I never have any luck growing chamomile ;-) Also, feverfew has a distinctly husky aroma.

Nigella is a very happy-to-grow-around-here flow. I love their frilliness and varying yet always intense shades of blue. I predict having tons more nigella next year as I am about to compost about a pound, maybe two of seed pods. If you want to know how happy nigella is to grow around here: they have overtaken the poppies.

Regarding the fennel: it is billowing up next to the blackberries (coming soon! – along with garlic and figs). I have often thought of fennel as invasive in the Southern California garden, but can you really call a plant invasive when you have planted it yourself? I know, right? My point being, if you don't hear from me for a while, it is probably because I have been overwhelmed by fennel.

MUSHROOM UPDATE:

Still no mushrooms! I have been trying to grow mushrooms in my backyard since December, and... nothing! However, I just joined the Los Angeles Mycological Society, and this outfit sounds like they know what they are doing. For example, yesterday I got an email from one of their trustees, welcoming me and calmly explaining why my dream of cultivating porcini mushrooms is virtually impossible. So now it is officially an impossible dream! I am looking forward to finding out what kind of mushrooms I can grow and share with you.

Made-Up Stuff

15

A Journey of Self-Discovery, Not a Maelstrom of Self-Loathing

Lionel pondered the first help-wanted ad he saw on Craig's List.

"Don't ponder!" a voice inside him shouted. "Just do. Go. Be!"

Lionel decided to name this voice Mr. Dogobe. It would be his friend and ally during the job search ahead. Job searches were grueling ordeals and you needed all the resources you could muster, very much including imaginary ones. Imaginary resources were in some ways preferable to actual ones, because they demonstrated resourcefulness and creativity – both desirable job skills.

This particular job — as a customer service representative for an on-line auction company – sounded potentially fascinating. Lionel could envision himself as the personification of the global economy. Part mascot, part trusted helpmate, like Jiminy Cricket or Batman's Robin. Lionel wondered if wearing a superhero outfit would be part of the job description. If not, he could suggest it – once he had learned the ropes. Employers liked employees who made suggestions. It demonstrated caring. They didn't like implementing suggestions, because that was too costly and anyway who did these employees think they were, questioning Standard Operating Procedures (S.O.P.)? But they liked the employees who made the suggestion, because it showed they were upbeat and involved and not spending every waking moment plotting the company's downfall.

This ability to see things both from management and worker's points of view was another thing that made Lionel so valuable as an employee. He should be keeping a list, so on a separate piece of paper he jotted down:

1. Imaginary inner resources
2. Makes suggestions
3. Management and worker POV

"That's three already!" Lionel marveled. "And I've only just begun." He had high hopes that his job search would prove truly to be a journey of self-discovery, not a maelstrom of self-loathing.

"Get on with it!" cried Mr. Dogobe, whom Lionel imagined as a little West Indian chap, dressed immaculately in white, sporting a sailor's cap.

Seeking only to oblige, Lionel scanned the rest of the ad. The Customer Service Representative was required to be intelligent, self-motivated, resourceful, well-organized, and detail-oriented."

"It's as if they know me!" Lionel murmured. A recent foray into bird watching proved his detail-orientation, and though it was perhaps not strictly job-related, it was a life experience he could mention anecdotally, allowing the wise interviewer to draw the smart conclusion.

Feeling himself enveloped by the universe's abundance, Lionel continued down the list of the job's duties and responsibilities. Only it was more than a job. He saw this clearly. It was a calling. He was going to put that into his cover letter.

"Don't!" warned Mr. Dogobe. "Just write a normal-sounding letter and spell-check everything."

It was good advice, and Lionel was glad to have it. In short order he had written up a concise cover letter listing how he had demonstrated the job's desired duties and responsibilities in an exemplary manner throughout his prior experience. Much (but not all) of this was imaginary, but that was okay because Lionel was drawing upon his inner resources – strength! – and also, he felt completely confident that he could cheerfully execute each of the requirements. Cheerfulness: that was a quality in short supply in the global economy. Lionel was ready to be the international ambassador of cheerful effectiveness. Just give him the chance.

Lionel found within himself the wherewithal to pen many such job applications – if five counted as many, which he felt strongly that it should, since five was two more than he thought he had in him. Three would be the max, he had assumed, but Lionel pressed himself. He exerted himself. He reached down deep, and then deeper, because he knew that this was a requirement of job seekers everywhere. You couldn't just pay lip service to the rigors of job-hunting.

Lionel knew that jobs – good jobs, satisfying jobs, soul-enriching jobs – did not just present themselves, like turkey vultures had at the beach, during his bird-watching phase. You had to work for them. You had to strip yourself down to the bare essentials, although not literally, especially not at an interview. But you had to be willing to put yourself out there in a way Lionel could not actually quite articulate, so for help he turned to Mr. Dogobe.

To his surprise and dismay, however, Mr. Dogobe was sound asleep, leaning with his back against the post of a pier. He appeared to be fishing. There was a fishing pole next to him with a line attached to a plastic ball bouncing up and down with the rippling tide. Up and down, up and down, up and down it bounced, while the tide rippled, and Mr. Dogobe did nothing but quietly snore.

It irritated Lionel to see his inner resolve sacked out like that, because there was a problem. The problem was, it was still only ten o'clock in the morning, and as heroic as Lionel's efforts had been, he still had twelve hours of consciousness ahead of him, which he had to fill up with something, somehow.

This was very daunting. It was one thing to be possessed of a divinely ordained conviction that you were going to change your life for the better, and another thing entirely to... um. Y'know. This was Lionel's point, exactly. What to do?

Napping would normally have been his first line of defense, in the hope that either being additionally well rested or having a dream would point him the way to go. However, he could not really justify a good snooze right at the moment; because first of all, at the end of that bird-watching phase, he had been the beneficiary of divine inspiration and he didn't want to come across to God as either unappreciative or needy.

Secondly, there was his imaginary avatar, already napping up a storm, and it would be unseemly for them both to be zonked out.

Left with no recourse, Lionel made the executive decision to go for a walk. He did this with neither haste nor undue deliberation. His tempo was like Goldilock's pick of porridge: just right.

Lionel held his chin up as he strolled. No. Not strolled! That implied leisure, and Lionel just now was a man of purpose –though of what purpose, he could not say... as he strode out into the morning sunshine, which struck him like the blast of a death ray.

Was he dying? Having a stroke? All Lionel knew was the sky was full of yellow-blue-white light, bearing down on him intent on annihilation. He covered his head with his arms and drew in his final breath, rich in oxygen, sweet oxygen, thank you oxygen for enriching every breath I've ever taken. I'm sorry it's only now, at this moment of ultimate surrender, that I...

As his gratitude increased, so did Lionel's awareness that as yet he remained seemingly intact. Was he in heaven? Not heaven? A parallel universe? Most likely, he thought with frantic re-assurance, it was none of these things, but rather he had simply jumped a track into an alternate version of his regular life. Usually such transitions were seamless and went unnoticed, but Lionel was possessed of heightened sensitivity due to his recent SFG (Sign from God).

Also, he noticed, as he patted the air at waist level all around him, instinctively seeking someplace to sit down, there were far, far fewer trees outside his apartment building than there used to be. Like, drastically fewer. And then it came back to him that management had been putting up signs for months that they were going to be chopping down the palm trees in front of the apartment because they were sick and dying and represented a big threat to topple over and kill someone, even though they looked perfectly healthy. The chopping-down must have happened while Lionel was in Baja, and he simply hadn't noticed while coming home at night, pre-occupied as he was.

He noticed now, though. Wow. What a difference. Without the usual canopy of palm fronds, the sky seemed twice as big. Lionel would not have been the slightest bit surprised if a spaceship appeared at that very moment, lowered its beam, and disgorged an army of giant robots. In fact, he was surprised when this didn't happen. All he heard was the rush of traffic going by on the freeway across the street, and all he saw was the fierce sunlight reflecting off the car bumpers with the insouciance of bullets that had missed him.

An indomitable feeling soon arose in Lionel.

"They can take away my palm trees, and yet I prosper. Still I thrive," he thought to himself. He had no thought of joblessness, no inkling of purposelessness. He was awash in his own irreducible essence. With each step, the sidewalk became more the instrument of his destiny. What this meant, he worried not.

At the end of the block he pressed the walk button and waited contentedly for his command to be carried out. As he waited, his eye lit upon a paper posted to the lamppost. It read, "Work at Home. Earn $1K/wk or more. Call to find out how."

Lionel's hand reached out toward the flyer and tore off the deed to his future, as effortlessly yet mightily as if pulling a sword from a stone.

"Hello. I'm calling about..."

"Yes. Excellent. Tell me more."

The voice was not too low and not too high, and steady, like the banister of a good staircase.

"I saw your work at home flyer, and I want to find out more."

"That's a big check for you in the Self-Starter box."

Lionel thought he could hear the squeak of a thick black magic marker, putting a check in a box. He wondered what other boxes were on the page and hoped they would all soon have a big thick check. He visualized this happening and felt brave.

"Can you tell me more about what the work entails?"

"Certainly. It entails making the world a calmer, healthier and happier place. How does that sound so far?"

"It sounds good but vague."

Lionel regretted the last comment. He should have thought of some way to phrase it positively. But you know what? He wasn't going to eat himself up over it. He was going to let it go, like a called first strike. Verbally striding into the silence, Lionel offered, "I'm curious to know more."

"Curious. Did you say curious?" The voice was welcoming as a witch who had just put on a cauldron to boil, but without evil intentions.

"I am curious," Lionel stated flatly.

"Curious is good. You need to be curious to succeed in this position. You need to wonder how many people will, if given the chance, grab onto a lifeline while they're drowning."

"Wouldn't everyone?"

"You'd be surprised." The voice spoke matter-of-factly. Lionel felt himself wishing he could simply state things the way they are, without longing, regret or fear. He decided he could, and would – starting right now.

"What's your name?" As soon as the words were out, he regretted them. He should have introduced himself, first. That would have demonstrated a better grasp of social conventions. He decided to instantly right any wrong he had committed, instead of worrying about it.

"My name's Lionel."

"Eddie. Glad to know you, Lionel. How do you feel about goats?"

"I wonder – do they really eat tin cans?"

"No, that's a myth. Goats are herbivores. They only eat plants. If they get hungry enough they'll eat almost any kind of plant, but we don't want our goats to get that hungry. Our goats are happy and we intend to keep them that way."

"So the job is about goats?"

"Fast learner. I just gave you another check."

"Does it involve feeding goats? The sign said work at home."

"The job involves feeding goats, but only indirectly. You would not have to feed them yourself unless you decided to avail yourself of the employee agricultural development program. That's where we bring you up to one of the farms for a week and give you an introductory course in goat-herding."

"Really?"

"Yes. It's the same course we give to inner city youths."

Half an hour later, Lionel was on the job.

The first thing you did when the member picked up was baa. When you baa'd, it cut through preconceived notions about telemarketing and went straight to primal communication. How did we all learn to talk? By imitating farm animals. Who hung up on telemarketers? Everyone. Who hung up on a talking goat? No one. Exactly! That's why you started off with a happy baa, like a goat who had just discovered a fresh clump of clover. If the member was having a problem at that moment with animal contentedness, well, so be it – but most people were okay with animal contentedness. It's what they craved, more than anything. That's what made this business such a winner.

So: "Baaa."

The silence on the other end was nothing unusual. You wanted silence. It showed the member was considering the initial proposition. What more could you want, one second into your presentation?

"Feeed meee."

These were familiar words. People knew what they meant. More important, members were used to hearing these words, coming from their own inner selves. Most often, it was Love the inner selves wanted. The ranking went like this:

1. Love
2. Knowledge
3. Sustenance

Those were the main three. Everyone could relate. As for the elongation of the vowel, the exaggeration of the long "e," that was simply more goat-like. You wanted members to be able to believe they were talking directly to a goat, not an intermediary. That captured the magic of trans-species communication, and you wanted all the magic you could muster. Members were captivated by the notion of talking to animals, as you could see by the widespread phenomena of having dogs not just as pets but as children, or by the habit of building theme parks as a pretext for worshipping dolphins as deities.

"What do you want?"

That was the desired first spoken response from the member. It was money. It was silver and gold. When the member voiced concern for *your* needs? Less than five seconds into the presentation? You felt the power then. You felt the nimbleness in your very haunches.

"I want to offer you a goat share."

Directness was the motto at this point. The member had expressed a desire to know what you wanted. Your responsibility was to fulfill the member's desire. Always fulfill the member's desire. AFMD.

"What in the world is a goat share?"

"No one expects you to buy an entire goat, even though they are very affordable. But, let me ask you this: what is your favorite part of a goat?"

Members loved being asked to name their favorites. That's why all professional sports had fans vote for the All-Star teams. The question drew them in. Also, the disclaimer about not being expected to buy the entire goat despite its affordability – that was simple parameter setting. Of course, you could buy the entire goat if you wanted. That was the Mountain Goat package, and it came with the shears and the bucket. It was hard for a member to receive the shears and the bucket and then not want to come to the farm. And once they came to the farm; well, then world calmness became appreciably closer, as did economic gratification for champions of sure-footedness. But it hardly ever happened that the member would immediately ask, "How much for the entire goat?"

What would happen, however, is they would tell you their favorite part of a goat, in this order:

1. Beard.
2. Smile.
3. Sure-footedness.
4. Horns.
5. Fur (or hair).
6. Clippity-cloppity sound of hooves.
7. Ability to eat tin cans.
8. Baaa.
9. Cheese.
10. Milk.
11. Meat.
12. Smell.

Any of these, except the one about the tin cans, was immediately sale-able. You just took whatever the member's favorite part was and asked how they'd feel about owning it. For example, "How would you feel about owning a premium goat's beard?"

And the answer – most gratifying to the telegoat-herd – would be, "I would feel happy about that."

Happy. Think about it. You had brought happiness into the members' life with a simple phone call. The rest of the call was confirmation of that happiness, and letting the member make the deal.

"How would you feel if I told you that you could own that goat's beard right now?"

"I'd feel great."

"What other questions do you have?"

"For how long?"

"For as long as you want."

"For how much?"

"Twenty dollars for the first two months."

"Can I do it for just one month?"

"There's a two-month minimum."

"How soon can I start?"

"You can start today."

"Do you need a credit card?"

"Yes."

With this sure-fire game plan in mind, Lionel made his initial "Baa."

The initial reply was, naturally, "Fuck you" and a hang-up. Nature gives a "Fuck you" and a hang-up to virtually all initial forays, just to see if you're really serious. Despite knowing this intellectually, the "fuck-you" still hurt Lionel's feelings, though he had promised Eddie he had a thick hide.

Nevertheless, Lionel persevered, because that was becoming part of his nature now. The second reply was "Baa" right back at him. In fact, this member would not stop baa'ing. Lionel was so nonplussed he forgot to say, "Feeed meee." They were just baa'ing at one another. Lionel felt an incipient kinship, but just as he and the member were getting into a rhythm, the call got cut off, and when Lionel called back, no one answered.

That meant his future must lie ahead, not behind, so Lionel called the third number and baa'd. This was met with silence. So far, so good.

"Feeed meee," Lionel bleated.

From the other end: hysterical laughter. It sounded like sneezing, hiccupping and gasping all mashed together. When the member recovered her breath, she said, "Whoever you are, thank you. Unless you're a crazy person. But even if you're a crazy person, I still thank you. I must be crazy myself, talking to a prank-caller pretending to be a sheep."

"It's a goat, ma'am," Lionel gently corrected, not wanting to take a risk by departing from the script. But what choice did he have? He couldn't telemarket a sheepshare. That would make no sense.

A fresh round of laughter ignited, this time louder, with more gasping. Lionel felt encouraged. He felt happy. He felt like he was making a friend.

"All right, Mr. Goat," said the member. "You have made my day and possibly my week. Tell me – what is it you want?"

They were back on script. Lionel went directly to directness: "I want to offer you a goat share."

"I accept," the member replied. "Can I get one for twenty dollars?"

"That's just right," Lionel said, improvising again. He sensed he would have to be doing a lot of this. "Will you be wanting to stroke its beard or hear its clomping hooves?"

"I want both."

"To get both is $30."

"All right. Thirty. Just don't upsell me any further, Goatman, or I won't be able to afford it, and that would spoil the precious thing we have together."

So, thirty dollars it was. Lionel had broken through. Not only had he made his first sale, he had also made his first upsell. Someone out there loved his goat voice so much she had to spend money to have it. That made Lionel feel real.

16

Bad Might Not Actually Be So Bad

The Creative Non-Fiction club consisted of Justin and Mr. Barker, alone together. This suited Justin splendidly because he could be as smart as he wanted without facing blowback from the nimrods. He could also come into Barker's class strumming, a troubadour in fact and deed. Mr. Barker might be grading papers, or reorganizing tardy slips and paper clips, or looking stunned: hands flat on desk, mouth-breathing, sea-glass green eyes scanning the horizon for non-forthcoming help.

Non-forthcoming except for Justin! He wanted to be playing his own song with his name in the title, like Bob Dylan's "Bob Dylan's Blues" or The Clash's "Clash City Rockers" or Shun the Doppelganger's "Ballad of Shun the Doppelganger." What was stopping him? Why not enter Mr. B.'s classroom with an eponymous song and a signature guitar lick a la "Folsom Prison Blues?"

Justin does not have a good answer for this. It is stacked up on a shelf with other hard-to-answer questions, including: how is he to restore his relationship with his father, if he is to restore it at all?; and does what transpired between himself and Suzanne count as making him a man, or must he do other things to be a man, and if so, what are they?; and why is he the only member of the Creative Non-Fiction club?

To avoid humiliating uncertainty, Justin approaches these questions in order of easiness-to-answer, even though none of them are easy.

Regarding being the only member of the club, Justin doesn't know what's up with the kids at his school. They flock to certain teacher's rooms at nutrition and lunch, congregating for who knows what reasons? How much is there to actually talk about?

Other than *Blood on the Tracks*, of course. Justin lately has been infinite-loop reading *Bob Dylan and the Making of Blood on the Tracks*. The story itself is a simple one. Dylan rescued himself mid-Seventies from a career nadir started by a mid-Sixties motorcycle accident caused proximally by his wobbly driving but more fundamentally by the unsustainability of his role as loquacious sphinx of the hippie generation. Dylan had crashed but not burned, fortunately. Burning is terrible and how people can self-immolate in protest like Mohamed Bouazizi, the street vendor in Tunisia who started the Arab Spring: that is really far, far beyond Justin's ken.

What might be more accessible is that period of Dylan ranging from *Nashville Skyline* to *Dylan*. How bad could it be? Justin has heard that Dylan covered Simon and Garfunkel's "The Boxer" during this period of his life. He would really like to know how Dylan handles the "lie-lie-lie" parts of that song, recorded when Dylan is said to have been concentrating on being a father. Many people name their sons Dylan, but how many sons name their fathers Dylan? Why is it that sons can't name their fathers? Especially when they get old and infirm? Or as in Justin's case, when a father has fucked up so royally as to need a new name capable of absorbing all of the fuck-up-ed-ness and yet still leave room for belief in a future.

With so many questions and no one to ask them, Justin enters Mr. Barker's room not at all strumming.

"How's it going today, Justin?" Mr. Barker says – but does he really mean it? Justin gives his favorite teacher the benefit of the doubt, not begrudging him the not-noticing of his guitar being encased and Justin not entering full troubadour.

Instead, Justin replies. "Bardically" – a last-minute line-up change; troubadour out, bard in. "Bob Dylan's father once rescued a man from a fiery car crash. He had polio, so he limped. Dylan's father, not the car crash victim. I don't know about the victim. It's like the Carter Family song, 'Wreck on the Highway,' except instead of praying, Dylan's father did something, like, save the guy's life. Do you know that song?"

"I do," says Mr. Barker, seemingly focused on a gleaming object out the window just beyond his field of vision, "but for some reason I can't bring it to mind."

"I have it on my phone," Justin says. Like most English teachers, Mr. Barker has pictures of his favorite writers on his walls, but instead of going wide, Mr. Barker has gone deep with pictures only of Gabriel *García Márquez,* Frederick Douglass, Emily Dickinson, and Esperanza So. Each adorns a horizontal strip seven feet up on a dedicated wall, at the same height as the pledge-thirsty flag. García Márquez and Douglass are featured in various stages of hirsuteness, focusing in García Márquez's case on robustness of mustache and insouciance of gaze; in Douglass's of outcropping of hair and jaw thrust. Dickinson has of course only the one photo, so Mr. Barker has magnified details: the full lips, the folded hands, the all-seeing eyes. As for So, he has reproduced the objects she uses in place of author photos: frozen grapes, levelled pencil erasers, footprints in sand.

"Here it is," says Justin. "The Louvin Brothers version." High lonesome harmonies mourn senseless loss of life. Justin joins in, head tilted back, neck pulsing. There are no rules against singing with students; in fact, it's encouraged -- so Mr. Barker also joins in, head tilted back, neck pulsing too. Voices connected in song is an important kind of connection. It definitely counts and can't be taken away. Remember that time we sang together? Everybody remembers that time. The question is, what to do when the song is over? A possible answer is: talk about it.

"I wonder if Dylan ever covered that song," Justin muses when "Wreck on the Highway" is over.

"He must have," Mr. Barker ventures. "He loves the Louvin Brothers."

"It's not a Louvin Brothers song, though. It's a Carter Family song."

Mr. Barker lets this go. He is practicing not having to be right, not having to untangle other people's self-evident contradictions that are not evident to themselves. What we have here is a kid with no one else to talk to, except me. I'm the one he's talking to. That says something... but what? Mr. Barker has questions of his own. They include: What are we here for? Are we validating one another's humanity? Is that a sufficient use of time?

Mr. Barker decides yes, it is; however, in addition to their talking to each other, Justin needs a project. Otherwise, the Creative Non-Fiction club is going to consist of Mr. Barker having lunch with one student, alone, every Tuesday, which would not be okay. Even this right here is barely borderline okay.

"Let's give you a project, Justin," says Mr. Barker.

"Okay, like what?" says Justin, both enthusiastically and defensively at the same time.

"I don't know," says Mr. Barker. "What are you interested in?" This is the standard question he asks to students who aren't noticeably interested in anything. Sometimes it catches them off-guard and gives Mr. Barker something to start with, a spindly seedling growing mostly flopped over on the ground. A spindly seedling is something to cultivate, that's Mr. Barker's point.

"What are you interested in?" is not quite the perfect question for Justin, who has an obviously keen interest in a certain Nobel Prize winning crooner; but this is lunchtime, not Perfect Time. And as if to vouchsafe every single thought bubble he has just interpreted from his only favorite teacher, Justin keeps the conversation going.

"I'm interested in Bad Dylan; specifically, the period from July 29, 1966, when he had his motorcycle accident, through the release of Blood on the Tracks on January 17, 1975, when everyone agreed he was a genius again. Did you know that Woody Guthrie, Dylan's idol – Dylan knew all of the words to all of Woody Guthrie's songs and actually sang them to Woody Guthrie while Woody Guthrie wasted away from Huntington's disease in a mental hospital near Morristown, New

Jersey in 1961 – I'm sorry I don't know the dates of the visits, but I can find out..."

"Please do," says Mr. Barker, so pleased by the momentary pause in data that he feels obliged to be encouraging, even though encouraging Justin to find out more about Dylan also feels like giving a bottle of vodka to an alcoholic.

"I will," Justin says. "It was definitely 1961, though. I also don't know if he ever visited Woody Guthrie again. Perhaps Dylan made his peace with Woody Guthrie, or perhaps Woody Guthrie gave him his blessing, or perhaps Woody Guthrie was so far gone that Dylan simply couldn't bring himself to visit again..."

"Or maybe he was just too busy?" Mr. Barker experiments with interrupting, just to see what will happen.

Justin knits his eyebrows together while pulling his head back. "Woody Guthrie had nothing but time on his hands by this point. His hands, by the way, had been so badly burned in a campfire accident in the early 50s that he could no longer play the guitar. He still wrote songs, however, and as the story goes, Woody Guthrie was going to leave all of his unpublished songs to Dylan for Dylan to record, but when Dylan went to visit Guthrie's house in Brooklyn, Guthrie's wife wasn't home, and Guthrie was in the mental hospital near Morristown, New Jersey, and the only person home was Guthrie's son Arlo, later to become famous for 'Alice's Restaurant' and less famous but still famous for 'Coming into Los Angeles' and 'City of New Orleans', but Arlo didn't know anything about any unrecorded music so Dylan left empty handed and that unrecorded music remained unrecorded until Guthrie's daughter Nora gave it to Billy Bragg and Wilco to record as Mermaid Avenue, which became a huge folk hit upon its release in 1998."

Here Justin pauses, to look first left, then right, and then cock his head and scrunch up his mouth.

Mr. Barker recognizes this as the look of a student who honestly wants to give an answer but cannot think of the words. He offers a prompt, but not the answer, because Mr. Barker himself does not know the answer and is curious to find out.

"So Bad Dylan refers to Dylan's being a bad person for not visiting Woody Guthrie more?"

"No," Justin says, with the freshness of an undersized trout returned to a glistening steam. "Bad Dylan refers to the poor critical reception received by Dylan's recorded output from 1967 through 1974. What critics and conventional wisdom fail to take into account is that Woody Guthrie died on October 3, 1967 at the age of only 55. And then, Dylan's father, Abram Zimmerman, died a mere six months later on May 29, 1968, at the age of only 56. People criticized Dylan for turning his back on the protest movement just when it needed him most, but I say the man had his heart full of private grief and deserved his period of mourning."

"That's very…" says Mr. Barker, but he can't think of the exact word to fill in the blank between "very" and "of you." He could say "obsessive" but that would be insensitive. He could say "empathetic," but what purpose is actually served by rendering judgment upon another person's behavior? Why not simply nod in the affirmative? Mr. Barker has just swung his jaw upwards and crinkled his eyes when Justin takes wing again, leaving Mr. Barker on the upstroke and having to dissolve his expression into neutral information-reception mode during the next outpouring.

"I just bought Self-Portrait, the album he recorded at the so-called nadir of his downturn. It was infamously reviewed in Rolling Stone by Greil Marcus, dean of Dylan critics, with the first line, 'What is this shit?' I haven't played it yet, though, because I'm afraid of how awful it might actually be. I'm afraid it might make me not like Bob Dylan and then I won't have anybody to be interested in. But I'm going to listen to it anyway because people have to face their fears. Everybody knows that."

Mr. Barker allowed himself a brief gaze into Justin's eyes, to determine if this outpouring had been rehearsed. The left eye pointed slightly toward the bridge of his nose, but the right eye was steady, and Justin's countenance overall appeared relaxed and spontaneous. There was always the issue with this student of the head seeming slightly too small to contain the face, like a balloon about to pop. However, this was an ongoing concern and not a reason to suspect Justin of preparing speeches beforehand. He was a kid with an especially pronounced interest in Dylan. More power to him. The key here was to find Justin some friends.

"I think Bad Dylan is a good topic," Mr. Barker says. "I'd be interested to hear more about what you discover."

"I know a lot more," Justin volunteers. "Did you know..."

"Probably not," says Mr. Barker, although he does know a fair amount, and part of him would like to find out if Justin has seen all or part of Renaldo and Clara. This is not the time to delve into Dylan's filmography, however. This is the time to change a young man's life.

"What I'm wondering is, do you think there are a lot of other kids at this school you could talk with about Dylan between Nashville Skyline and Blood on the Tracks?"

"Probably not," says Justin cheerfully. "But why would I have to talk to anyone here about it? It's good that nobody else is a Dylanologist. It's what makes me distinctive. You have to be distinctive to get into college."

"That's true," says Mr. Barker, giving credit where it's due, but not allowing himself to get sidetracked by the endorphins produced whenever a student spoke sensibly about college. Instead, he says exactly what he means. "What if your project involved finding something to talk about other than Dylan?"

Justin openly smirks. "What else is there?"

"That sounds like a good question for you to investigate."

"You want me to walk up to people and ask them what they like to talk about?"

"Is that not a good idea?" asks Mr. Barker. To him it seems like an excellent idea. He imagines Justin gaining all manner of insight.

Becoming well-rounded. He could transform himself from an obsessed youth into a budding journalist. A rock journalist, if they still existed. Mr. Barker would be happy to add that to his lifetime ripple effect.

"It's not a bad idea," says Justin. "I'm just not sure that I want to do it."

"Why do you have to be sure?" asks Mr. Barker.

"Because I don't like people making fun of me," says Justin.

This is a reasonable objection. In fact, it's the most reasonable objection Mr. Barker can think of. He is always teaching his students to anticipate objections and treat them respectfully before refuting them. Treating objections respectfully shows you're a reasonable person.

"That's a reasonable objection," Mr. Barker says. "What about if we did it together? You could say it was my project and you're helping me for extra credit."

"Okay," Justin says. He takes his food tray, puts it in the trash, and heads out the door. He's going to try it right away, while it's still lunch time.

He sees a girl in the hallway, a really short girl with a grow-up face. He has often though she seemed wise, like a 75-year-old teenager. He says to her, "Excuse me, but I'm working on a project for the Creative Non-Fiction club. Mr. Barker asked me to ask people, what is easy for them to talk about."

"So you want to know what I like to talk about?" says the girl.

Justin nods.

"Well, I like to talk about shopping. I like to talk about food." She pauses, looks up, thinks of more things. "Movies. Make-up. Music. The three M's! Do I have to talk to you about each of them as part of your project?"

"Yes," Justin decides.

"Okay, which one first?"

Justin is afraid she won't like his kind of music, so he says, "Make-up."

"Okay, what about it?"

"What's your favorite kind?"

"That's a really good question. I think I would have to say fingernail polish, because there are so many colors and it's also very pampering of yourself to put on and take off fingernail polish. You can't be in a hurry. It's like meditation other people can see."

The girl wiggles her light pink nails in front of Justin's eyes, so he can admire them.

"Meditation you can see," he says.

"Exactly!" she says, sounding as pleased as if she had gotten a hard answer right on a test. "You can ask me more make-up questions later, but now I've got to go."

"Okay," Justin says, stunned by the simplicity of it all. "When?"

"Whenever," says the girl. "We always pass in the hall. Think of another question to ask the next time you see me. My name's Sylvie. Bye!"

Justin is staggered by his success. You can find out about people just by asking them questions! This is incredible.

The next person he finds is a boy, a stocky kid with an almost-grown mustache and sad eyes. He tells the boy about his project and asks his question. The boy replies, "I could talk about playing football, or about video games."

Justin hates football and video games almost equally, but he hates video games slightly less, so the choice is easy. All he has to do is say, "Tell me about video games. Why are they easy for you to talk about?"

"I don't know," the boy says, but then promptly proves that he does. "There's a lot of action, they're not boring, I can tell when I'm getting better and my friends are really interested in it so we talk about them and learn from each other. It's fun."

"You learn from each other," Justin repeats.

"Yeah, like how to get to new levels and exchange weapons, that kind of stuff."

"Cool," says Justin. "Thanks.

"Do you want to ask me about football?"

"I will the next time we meet," says Justin. "I see you all the time in the halls." This is not technically true regarding the past, but Justin is certain it will be true regarding the future. When he gets home, he goes right to his room and writes down his conversations with Sylvie and Kevin. He also listens to and immediately writes his review of *Self-Portrait*. He can't wait to find out what Mr. Barker has to say about it. The title is "Bad Might Not Actually Be So Bad."

17

The Boy Without a Song

The rent-a-car lurched as if it too anticipated a fatal collision immediately upon exiting the prison access road.

"Whoa," Justin said from the back seat as the passenger-side tires returned to earth with a jolt and a thud.

"be QUIET!" his mother admonished him so severely that neither he nor his just-released father ventured to comment on how, in the southbound fast lane, the car was now stopped.

She was breathing hard without making any sound, but the tendons sticking out in her neck stated plainly that she was waiting for a corrections officer to come sprinting after them waving papers showing it was all a mistake: Eric hadn't been paroled after all, they had gotten him confused with someone else's husband and father. Or, there were library fines. A piece was missing from the commissary chess set, meaning that he would have to start all over again except this time without parole.

Or, she was waiting for the 18-wheeler with their name on it.

Justin surprised himself by having not a care in the world. His dad was out of prison so everything was fine. He celebrated the moment by contemplating the short stone barrier between the north and southbound lanes. Limestone blocks interconnected for as far as the eye could see, past his mother's quivering knuckles, through the smeared and splattered windshield and way on uphill to a bend in the road. Some rectangular blocks horizontal, some blocks vertical, other blocks square or irregular. Someone had figured out how they all fit together.

Several silences later, Eric cleared his throat in such a way as to let Laylin, Justin, God, America and people listening overseas know he intended to speak.

"I have some goals I'd like to share with you," Eric intoned. His voice sounded like an artifact in a museum, on display its own glass case with special lighting: a deep, smooth, round bowl crafted from granite and gold, used solely for the ritual of setting forth life-after-prison goals.

"I want to invent something new that helps people connect face-to-face, involving eye contact. I want to make restitution to the Jeffries family. And I want to be the father and husband our family needs."

His father's shoulders relaxed, as if he had made a speech in school and now whatever grade he got didn't matter nearly so much as the fact that the speech was over.

Justin also imagined, although he couldn't see, his father's eyes darting around, trying to catch sight of the genie who would now be in charge of granting these wishes. This was pathetic and could not be allowed to continue. He felt confident, however.

God would tell him what to say.

He waited, and waited.

Then God spoke.

"Don't say anything. Roll down your window and let the wind drown out what he just said. Then put on your headphones. Crank it and let him hear that you're not listening. That will show him he doesn't get to just come out of prison and immediately start calling the shots."

This sounded vengeful, which also made Justin feel it was really God talking. However, at that moment, they passed a sign for Cal Poly Compost on the other side of the road, so now he wasn't so sure. It would be rude to ask God to show you a sign while He was in the middle of talking to you, so Justin kept his eyes open, and sure enough, they passed under a blinking yellow light, supposedly warning that a stoplight was coming up, but Justin knew it meant that ultimately, he was going to have to make up his own mind.

In his mind, Justin said, "Thank you, God."

The freeway roared and Justin rode inside the belly of the whale until they reached downtown San Luis Obispo, where the whale spat Justin back onto the backseat of the car. His mother had missed the turnoff and the GPS was frantically re-routing as she ignored its directions.

"May I suggest…" was as far as Eric got.

"You may not," Laylin cut him off.

Eric turned his head to the right, where the freeway and his freedom must continue. He looked partly wistful, a natural look, emphasizing the sparkle in his eye, which Justin was glad to see prison had not extinguished, only diminished. He also looked impassive, like a little kid who knew he wasn't tall enough to go on the grown-up ride at an amusement park and that no amount of fit-pitching would fix. It was both humiliating and comforting for Justin to experience his father as being mature for a six-year-old.

Meanwhile, Santa Rosa Street was way too wide for the few cars travelling on it. Justin knew the name because it was written on the street sign in fancy script which he couldn't decide if he liked or if it was pretentious. Low trees, low roofs and low hills all bowed down to a sky the same color as the pavement.

To Justin's immediate right was a brick storefront with a sign that read "Wild Side Smoke Shop." It looked like a party supply store without the party. The windows themselves were smoked, so that Justin could see his own reflection, the pensive boy with the round head and clean part, who looks like he's going to the vet to see his dog put to sleep. Below his reflection he read "ALL OTHER SMOTKING ACCESSORIES."

He wondered what it would be like to be the Smot King. It depended on what Smot was. Taking all the fun out of it as had become her speciality, his mother said, "I hate this town. Is anybody hungry? The first place you see, just shout out. I don't care."

How could she not care? It was going to be their first meal together. She must care more than she could bear to say. Justin tried to hear the passion buried within her indifference. To do this, he would have to make her speak about something she felt passionate about. This required considerable deliberation, which took Justin out of the moment until bam, there they were inside a fancy cafeteria with an assembly line where workers rapidly and precisely assembled scrumptious platters behind a sanitary glass barrier.

"What are *your* goals, Mom?" Justin asked, nonchalantly as a beagle speaking Portuguese.

"We're still talking about goals?" replied Laylin, who still had her sunglasses on.

"Dad said his, and I've been thinking about mine. I'm curious about yours." His parents were displaying contrasting attitudes towards their salads. Eric appeared to be having a divine revelation of his own, while Laylin seemed to be detecting powerfully magnified mites and aphids. Justin himself felt normal. Figuring out your goals apparently produced a calming effect. He thanked God for the idea, which gave him another idea.

"Let's say grace."

His mother looked at him as though he had proposed they recite *Mein Kampf*. His father had damp cheekbones. Before either of them could argue, comment upon or improve his idea, Justin said, "Thank You God for bringing our family safely back together, and thank You also for this food we're about to eat."

As Eric took his first bites of free man's food, he was power-chomping while sighing. Years of degradation washed away like blood down the shower drain.

Laylin watched attentively, as if she had accidentally tuned in to a riveting nature documentary. A flicker of amusement was gone before it fully happened. Then her facial façade crumbled. She looked old in time that couldn't be counted by years. Her eyes showed the concern they would have shown for any animal about to be overtaken by a predator. Her mouth opened slightly in preparation for an expression of grief. Justin could see her eyeballs flick up and right, up and left, sideways, sideways, down. With each rejected choice she withdrew another order of magnitude further away, from treetops to horizon to the limits of earth's atmosphere to the orbit of Mars to beyond and beyond and beyond.

"Mom," Justin said, to bring her back. "What are your goals?"

The message took a long time to travel through space. Meanwhile Eric put his fork down after every bite. He drank water between bites, from a thick pint glass dense with condensation and rivulets. He kept saying, "This is good."

Laylin finally sent back a message. She said, "I want us all to get home safely."

"That's a good goal," Justin said, surprised to hear himself speak in a voice that did not noticeably alarm any of the other diners, and to see himself not reaching across the tablecloth to shake his mother by her strong shoulders. "Would you like to set any that are longer-term?"

"Not at the moment," she replied. "Except we should all use the bathroom before we leave. I don't want to have to stop again."

Justin shifted tactics. He attempted to use telepathy to make "Stand by Me" by Ben E. King and/or "Bring it On Home to Me" by Sam Cooke and Lou Rawls come up on his mother's inner soundtrack, but she was beyond soundtrack. Justin nevertheless attempted to transmit "Let's Stay Together" back-to-back with "I'm So Tired of Being Alone" by Al Green, like an emergency room doctor continuing to perform CPR on a patient long expired.

"Stop looking at me like that," she told him.

"This is so good," said his father.

Two hours later, Justin looked out from his mind to see their rented bungalow, a stunted mushroom. Wood chips in the front yard were the remains left over by a marauding army. There were saving graces, however. A brand-new picket fence, not white, still-unpainted wood, promised to do its best to ward off further intrusion. A progression of palm trees spindly as giant dandelion puffs offered testimony that someone, at some time, had cared about making things nice. So did the fact that every single house on their street was a bungalow. Bungalow, bungalow, bungalow, bungalow: once upon a time, there had been a plan. However unoriginal it may have been; still, it was a plan.

Furthermore, twilight restored color to the sun-bleached street. Even the dehydrated green of their own house took on a temporary pistachio glow. Some luggage would have helped give Justin something to do; however, his father had been released with nothing. Not a suitcase, not a spindle, not a trash bag. He had his involuntary man-slaughtering hands to carry. With nothing of his father's to hold and only his head-phones to weigh him down, Justin felt like he might float away like the one balloon a birthday boy had really wanted to save.

It was worse than awkward to be coming home to a place that wasn't home and didn't even have a welcome home sign. It didn't need to be a banner, but it should have been something. It was too sad for his father to be coming back to nothing.

"Wait here," Justin commanded. In a way this might be perfect. He could leave his parents alone for a moment that could turn out to be the magic moment. Some tiny gesture, Justin didn't know what – the upturn of a wrist? A misplaced kiss landing on neck instead of lips and by its very waywardness finding the way home?

Justin sprinted up the walkway, did not trip on the steps, broke right on the patio like a halfback evading tacklers, and opened the intricately carved door with his very own key.

Now the question became: where, oh, where could he find a blank sheet of paper? Things that were not blank sheets of paper taunted him. Sofa cushions. Thermostat. Clock.

Desperation led Justin to a moving box with its top flaps open. In-side were measuring cups, wax paper, rolling pins. There was no time to make pie. He tore off one of the flaps of the moving box and there he had it: a sturdy thing to write on. Now he needed something, anything to write with. Red kettle on black stovetop: no! Wine rack stocked with bottled water: no! He thought he spied a pencil on the not-real-granite counter but it was a grape stem.

It was then that the Miracle of the Sharpie occurred. What had not been there when first he glanced over the counter now was made manifest. Good ol' black Sharpie, cap on, inked up, good to go. Harps, trumpets, church organs, fog horns, children's choirs all exalted. Maybe Justin was overreacting with all the music references but he couldn't really help it. That's how he reacted.

Moments later he stood in the doorway with a bona fide Welcome Home sign. The necessary materials had presented themselves. You couldn't extrapolate too much from this, but you could extrapolate something. It was like winning on Opening Day.

His mother and father both smiled warmly, authentically. There. See? The impossible was possible. It was all in how you thought about it. No. It was all in what you did about it.

"Are you going to let us in?" teased his mother, the teaser.

"What's the password?" he teased her back.

"Freedom," his father answered correctly, sounding convinced of his own existence for the first time. He seemed to be sizing Laylin up for to carry her over the threshold. Perhaps he was sizing her up in general. That was allowed. As his parents proceeded into the kitchen, his father taking in the environs with wide eyes but no comment, Justin removed himself into the living room to give them a little much-needed privacy in the kitchen.

Justin hoped he would soon have to go on a long walk, although a bus ride seemed more advisable than a tromp around this neighborhood after dark. Not that he was afraid, except, he was, even more so when he heard his mother plainly state, "I can understand how you would feel that way, but I have to be honest and tell you I'm just not ready."

"You don't have to be honest," his father replied. All music ceased. "You could pretend."

Justin could only see their torsos, and that was too much. He diverted his eyes to the sofa. Its cushions were wrinkled and the fabric gathered up, as though the sofa had recently lost a drastic amount of weight.

His father said something too soft for Justin to hear, to which his mother responded, "Please do not say another word to me about Kris Kristofferson, ever."

Justin could see a section of the refrigerator, shining as if buffed to remove all traces of fingerprints. It repelled his gaze to the also-gleaming gooseneck faucet over the unstained sink, where there were three pump dispensers of soap: cotton candy pink, skim milk white, save-the-planet clear. The beige paper towel holder was empty, its stubby arms leaning in as if wanting to console each other but unable to connect.

"You keep telling me what not to do," his father said. "May I ask what you would like me to do?"

"Do we really have to do this right now? He's listening, you know."

There was no miracle miraculous enough to save this situation. Justin discovered his Welcome Home sign was still in his hands. He took long steps to the front door and flung it into the yard, in such a way that entirely by accident it swooped up like a flying carpet, then paused, reconsidered, and fluttered to rest face up on the still warm ground.

Justin turned around and Eric was standing there.

"What are you gonna do?" Justin asked.

"I'm going to invent something new that helps people connect face-to-face, involving eye contact." He himself was not making eye contact, however. He was staring up into his brain to remember the rest of this speech, which sounded less confident the more it sank in the non-prison air. "I'm going to make restitution to the Jeffries family. And I'm going to be the father and husband our family needs."

"Welcome home," the prostrate sign still said, like the dying words of a fallen horseman.

Shaggy-haired, deep-eye-socketed Neil Young glared at Justin from the poster on his wall, angry at him for not being able to warble all of his emotions into music. Yet despite Neil's harshness, Justin gave himself credit for making progress on getting his index finger down to cover the first two strings just about the first fret. He was definitely producing more music and less mistake. Justin knew better than to expect Neil to give him any credit, though.

In order to feel better, he practiced no song. Instead he played the F chord 16 times, then practiced changing from C to F 16 times. Sometimes the F sounded like a short circuit crackling in a fuse box before the entire panel starts shooting out sparks. Other times it sounded simply like metal wires being plucked. Increasingly, however, it sounded good and warm, like music. Justin felt he should be making up a country song but didn't feel anything coming on. He was the Boy Without a Song, which made him feel sadder, which made him even more want to put his feelings into words. Still, nothing came to him, until he started adding in G.

G was dependability: sunrise, church bells. No matter how sad he felt, Justin could strum a decent G. And as he played C, C, F, F, G, G over and over, he started hearing two songs: "The First Cut is the Deepest" and "Wild Thing." To Justin's ear, his slow and cautious rendition sounded exquisitely heartfelt, with the words about wanting to give love another chance even though the singer is permanently damaged by an earlier relationship sounding true, true, true. Not really being able to sound the full F chord experience every single time gave his rendition an unpredictable lo-fi truth, Justin thought. It was his first original medley arrangement and he felt proud of his voice feeling sore with emotion, until he realized his father was listening in the doorway.

It was like looking at a statue of a fallen tyrant. But it was also like looking at the person Justin loved and missed so much it was terrible, and it wasn't even like that. It was that.

His father had shadows under his eyes that looked more convincing than his sandcastle smile. His formerly thick hair had thinned out but could still be combed over without looking like too much like a combover, despite his overly wrinkled brow, which looked like he had been given think-too-much pills. What kept Justin from combusting out of combined mortification and pity was his father's black t-shirt with no logo. That's what he always wore before he went to prison and apparently this was one way in which he had not changed. He looked like a public service announcement about how serving time would make a once confident-to-the-point-of-cocky person look decrepit and defeated, even if he could manage to eke out a half-smile of modest pride in something he had no business taking any pride in.

This all made Justin's sore throat much worse, but he had to plunge ahead because that's what you do once you start plunging. He was glad to be mumble-singing even though this was futile in terms of hiding what he was saying because his father had taught him the words.

Somehow "The First Cut is the Deepest" managed to hold up and maintain recognizable form until the end of the chorus. It was an indestructible song like "Four Strong Winds," which Justin made the spot-decision that he would learn next. His father had taught him that a cement mixer and garbage truck could sing "Four Strong Winds" as a duet and it would still sound good. He could not unlearn the things his father had taught him just because his father had involuntary manslaughtered a boy only a few years older than Justin, with many similar interests. The fact that his father had done something horrible and irreparable to that boy and his family did not mean that Justin had to do something horrible and irreparable to himself. This was a thought that happened inside Justin's head so many times it was happening all the time. He was aware of it at some times more than others and right now he was extremely aware of it. It felt like someone struggling to keep his own hands from tightening around his own neck.

This was where he lost track of which chord was supposed to go with which words and which fingers went with which chords. In the confusion, his father got away from the door frame and came lurching towards Justin like Frankenstein. Justin tried to drive him back by thrashing out the "Wild Thing" riff, but his playing had disintegrated into bashing and then nothing. Eric held out his arms in such a way as to make plain that it was his turn to hold the guitar.

Justin wanted to scream or cry but there was no way to sink into the floor or disappear or save himself. All he could do was feel the pain of seeing his father being out of prison and that still not making him feel better, which meant nothing ever would.

"Let me show you something I learned in prison," his father said. Even in the depth of despair, Justin had to admit this was a compelling introduction. It might possibly work for Justin in an as-yet unformed future to go around telling people, "Here's something my father taught me that he learned in prison."

Even though all of his father's fingers were technically there, they were diminished. Boney, not meaty. His wedding ring visibly wobbled as he lowered himself to sit cross-legged about six inches away, smelling clean and dry but stale from his black t-shirt that hadn't been worn in years. Tendons flared on his hands as he strummed and tuned, making Justin feel guilty for not having tuned up perfectly. Now it was too late.

"F chord, right? That's the tough one. You're doing a good job."

His father's praise shined a searchlight from the base of Justin's spine into all the chambers of his heart. He searched there for instructions on how to put his family back together, like a poster of what to do in a restaurant when someone's choking.

Oblivious to the commotion, his father's eyes sparkled and their outer corners crinkled. His dimples turned the sparkles sparklier and crinkles crinklier and made him believable. "Watch what happens when you keep your fingers the same and slide them up the neck one fret."

His dried glue hands became wizard hands.

"F sharp," he announced while strumming a strong chord suitable for heralding the entrance of a prince. Justin felt gravity loosen as a direct result of his father going up the neck. It felt like weight lifting not only from his shoulder blades but also from behind his eyes, and from his hamstrings, the balls of his feet, his ball balls, and also the lining of his stomach. Everything in and around him fit together five percent better and felt ten percent stronger.

"G," his father proclaimed. Justin had always wondered about the neck, and here was his un-imprisoned father, teaching him.

"A good song for practicing this technique would be 'Me and Julio Down by the Schoolyard,'" his father said, making eye contact.

"I love that song," Justin responded, focusing on to his father's perceptibly less scrunched forehead, like someone in the beginning stages of returning to human form after a curse had turned them into a mute beast. To win a staring contest, focus on the forehead. This was also something his father had taught him, and here it was, coming in handy.

El Lanzamiento Viene

18

Gritty All Day Long

Most of the other baseball players at the Pacific Coast League tryouts were half my age. Nobody said the league was for guys in their twenties, but that was the deal. Some goofuses showed up in shorts and tennis shoes. Not me, though. I own four different pairs of baseball pants. I didn't have on cleats, however. I was getting by with turf shoes, because I had not yet earned the exalted status bestowed by cleats. It really makes a difference to have your feet a quarter inch off the ground. Also, the clackety-clack of cleats on concrete is clear confirmation that you are a ballplayer, not a hapless schmo just going through the motions.

I thought it was a sure thing I would be drafted, probably drafted high. Everybody needed a fifty-seven-year-old catcher who hadn't played in twenty-five years — and who, on the late-August day of tryouts, was still seeing double from brain damage in April. Not severely double right in front of me. I'd been able to teach high-school English up until the AP exam in mid-May and then take medical leave. But double, as in: Isn't it weird how the walls are intersecting twenty feet down the hallway, and the students and the lockers and the floors are all looking more than a little bit swervy?

The trick, which I learned after going back to playing tennis in early August, was to keep the ball in front of you. If you let the ball get in on you, you (a) lose power and control and (b) have to pick which one of the two balls to hit.

My brain damage was not from a stroke, by the way. It was a "cavern-ous malformation" that leaked in my brain stem: a blob of blood-vessel cells that never quite form veins nor arteries nor capillaries; a vascular Creature from the Black Lagoon of your brain. You could have one and never know, like I did, until one day a little mutant blood vessel inside my brain stem suddenly oozed some goop. If the brain is like a computer, then this is like spilling coffee on your keyboard. I can't say what your keyboard feels, but I felt whacked by a two-by-four that didn't hurt but left me seeing some

serious double

and also

a little

wobbly, what

with that

numbness in

my left

leg,

from foot

to calf.

For a while there, the tingling went all the way up my thigh and into my balls, which was alarming, but, still, it could have been much, much worse.

I slept a lot. Deeeeeep sleeeeeeep. My wife was *very upset* and dem-onstrated her love in both conventional and unconventional ways. For example, she went two-for-two in passing out during my initial medical exams — first in the emergency room and then again a few days later at the neurologist's office. If that's not love . . . well, it is.

She also did not yell at me one single bit when, fitted out with prism glasses, I backed my car out of the driveway and scraped her Volvo up nicely. Not a peep.

It is true that she was *very concerned* about how mean I was to her during this period. I wrote her two poems explaining that I wasn't being mean, but she wasn't buying it. For evidence of my meanness you will have to read her essay, if she ever writes one. What I felt was grateful and eager to recover so she would not feel meanness but rather l-o-v-e.

Over the course of my medical leave and summer vacation the tingling retreated back the way it came, down the quads and the calves and then around the ankle to one last holdout in my left foot, which still sometimes tingles to this day — my own personal memento mori, disconcerting but not enough to keep me sidelined. It's a reminder, if you will, to do it now, whatever *it* may be. In my case *it* was playing baseball — actual hardball, not softball — with seventeen other guys and an ump and uniforms. The real thing.

I thought tryouts went great. I played catcher, just catcher. You may ask, How solid was my receiving with that lingering double vision? Well, I'm happy to report that squatting behind the plate was a miracle cure. I saw completely normal and snagged a whole lot of balls in the dirt. Each time I did, I was like: Looky here, pure gold. That whooshing hardball crashing into the grit, chaos about to explode, but no! My mitt swooped down and snagged it, and a satisfying *thunk* transmitted deep satisfaction direct from the web of the glove to the left prefrontal cortex.

Of course, plenty of balls also skipped right by me, but these were mainly wild pitches — i.e., the pitcher's fault, not mine. At least, according to me. I'm not really into whose fault it was. Let's just say a nontrivial number of pitches had destinies other than being caught. That feels like the truth. I also made no attempt whatsoever to field any pop-ups behind the plate. Too many balls lying around back there; you could break an ankle. In retrospect maybe I should have jumped up, turned around, and flung off my mask before I looked in dismay at the scattered balls and reluctantly abandoned what would have for sure been a dogged, ultimately triumphant pursuit.

To be honest, I cannot recollect ever in my entire life catching a foul pop fly as catcher, but I was in no mood to let such obvious limitations hold me back. There were about a hundred guys who needed to hit and just me and one other, obviously way-better-than-me guy taking turns behind the plate. This guy was Robo-Catcher, but perfectly friendly.

He was like, Go ahead, and I was like, No, you go ahead. Me and Robo took turns. He was younger, of course, and I knew if it was just between him and me, he'd get picked first. But I could live with that.

On my turn catching I was very encouraging to all the batters: "Whoa, dude, you nailed that one." One batter, built like a rustic cabin, swatted a ball that dented the outfield fence. *Ka-blam!* Another guy — jitteriest person I ever saw in my entire life, a downed power line in human form — batted lefty and made plenty of contact. This guy had eye-black all over his cheeks: an impressively deranged look.

In my own at-bats I got some hits, nothing Ruthian but nevertheless undisputed line drives to the outfield. I had no regrets. I did what I'd set out to do. Solid contact — that's my brand. When you need a line drive up the middle, call me.

After everyone had hit, it was time for the managers to pick, which was done playground style — brutal, merciless, fair: pick the best guys first, then the middle guys, and then we'll just have to see. Everybody needs a catcher who can hit, I thought. This is going to be redemptive. Watch me now.

And yet when the picking started, the coaches didn't pick me, and they didn't pick me, and they didn't pick me. Time slowed. My heart-beat amplified. All these other guys were getting picked, but not me. At first it was humbling, and then it was alarming. What if I didn't get picked at all? I had told all my students I was trying out. What would I say to them? It was too harrowing a thought to consider. The possibility of not getting picked blotted out everything except the green, green grass while I contemplated the question of whether to stand up straight, or lean against the fence, or gradually disappear.

I became full of mercy for the outcasts of the world. In the future I would treat them with compassion, show an interest, listen to their stories. In particular when kids failed in my classroom, I wouldn't secretly roll my eyes in exasperation: No! Never again. I couldn't go back and change the past, but from now on I could and would be kinder to the not-good-enough.

Then I got picked.

This tall, sad-eyed guy, who a couple of months later would hit two grand-slam home runs in the same game, approached me unnoticed (so preoccupied was I with how to stand) and said, with what in retrospect sounds like a note of apology for the long wait, "Hey, do you want to play with us?"

Whatever I actually said, what I felt was: *Whoop whoop!* I shed all trepidation like a snakeskin as I followed my new manager back to the chosen circle, leaving behind the remaining half dozen or so not-yet-and-maybe-never-picked players. One guy, as old as I am if not older, kept tossing the ball into his mitt: *thump, thump.*

I wonder even now what I would tell that guy, if I could tell him something encouraging but real. I keep thinking about that guy, who could so easily have been me; who, let's face it, *is* me in the alternative universe we all know is right there waiting for us whenever we don't catch a lucky break.

Among my instantly beloved teammates I recognized the cabin-sized guy who had hit the mightiest clout of tryouts, and the hyper guy with eye-black spread all over his cheeks. A guy with a long black beard told me there was a pitcher on our team who could throw ninety-plus miles per hour, and I should get ready for my hand to hurt.

This was the best news I'd ever heard, although it turned out not to be true. That guy maxed out in the high seventies. Also I was our team's fourth-string catcher, which is really not a thing unless you make it one, which you must do if you are to be true to your inner game. So I hung on to that role and played maybe twenty-something innings over a fourteen-game season. I could see where things were headed early on and floated a complaint about it to my wife, who said, "As long as they let you play sometimes and you have fun, it's OK," so I went with that.

I did not see a ton of action, but I also did not see none, and furthermore I made a contribution. From the dugout with the other subs I did a lot of hooraying for our side and also talked some pretty vicious trash about the other team. Everyone plays a role.

We went undefeated and won the championship by a wide margin in a game in which I did not play at all. Yet there was one midseason game where none of the other three catchers could make it. So, yeah, I caught all nine innings, ending with us up 3-2. When you win 3-2, you know the catcher had to have been doing something right, and that was me, with a hand on the ground behind home plate so I wouldn't keel over but rather maintain a steady squat. *If this is where I go from a malformed blood vessel, then bury me right here.* That was my exact thought. It kept me going through innings seven, eight, and nine.

I am not going to tell you that I was a stellar catcher. Gritty, sure. Gritty all day long. But now I know: Those balls that get by you in practice? They also get by you in a game, and while a couple of passed balls here and there is OK, more than a couple is not. I got taken out of one game, mid-inning. With the bases loaded we got the runner out at third, and the throw home was there in my mitt, then gone. That was a real gut-clencher.

I told my students about it the next day. What's the point of failure if you don't make use of it? We share personal news at the start of each class, to get off on a human note before I tell them to put their headphones away. So I told them about being taken out in the middle of the inning, and nobody said anything. The room was still. The moment lingered.

This was the one game where my wife was watching. The games were way out in the wilds of the San Fernando Valley, but my wife came to this game on a sunny Sunday morning with sunglasses and dimples glinting, and you know what she said?

That I looked like a ballplayer.

I think that's what I would tell that unpicked guy thumping the ball into his mitt back at tryouts. I would tell him he's a ballplayer for sure.

19

The Orange Appreciation Award

I wanted to make fresh-squeezed orange juice for my former neighbor from Austin, who now lived in Milwaukee and was visiting with her two kids after her husband had died from pancreatic cancer. A kind man and father who'd played accordion in beer gardens on weekends was dead. Fresh-squeezed, backyard orange juice was going to be my expression of sympathy for his widow and her preteen son and daughter. Then something went wrong. I got out the ladder, but I didn't pick any oranges. Did I get a cramp and become unable to climb? I don't remember. I do know I was pretty depressed when my old neighbor and her kids came to visit. My own dad had just died. My daughters had left for college. My high-school students did not love me. Making fresh orange juice was going to be that thing where you do a good deed for someone who's feeling even worse than you, partly to help that person feel better, but just as much or even more to make yourself feel better.

Instead of making orange juice, I took my former neighbors to Dockweiler Beach. It's underrated due to planes from LAX taking off directly overhead and the sewage-treatment facility nearby. Still, it's a beach with little traffic, easy parking, ocean, sand, birds, lifeguard stands, and people all pursuing beach bliss in their own ways. We sat in our street clothes on a blanket, which brought us closer than if we'd been sitting on individual beach towels. I should describe the family, but they're real people with real feelings. Let me just say that they had sadness on the outside, their regular selves in the middle, and more sadness inside, so that looking at them was like trying to adjust a camera that zooms in and out of focus.

It was about sixty-one degrees, the minimum possible beach temperature, but these guys were on spring vacation from still-frozen Wisconsin, so sixty-one degrees was a blessing. They enjoyed being at the beach. You could tell by their relaxed smiles and how they leaned toward the sun.

Even I, who hate the beach — there's nothing to do, and sand gets in your books — set aside my grievances and enjoyed their enjoyment. The day didn't go according to my plan, with all of us sipping orange juice and saying, "Ahh," and feeling assuaged. It went even better, according to no plan at all: just me saying, "Hey, do you want to go to the beach?" and them saying, "Sure."

2

I keep a few backyard oranges mixed in with the baseballs in the bucket I take to practice. Every time one of my teammates peeks in, he's like, "Oranges?" question mark, when it really ought to be "Oranges!" EXCLAMATION POINT!

My teammates are regular guys. One is studying Swedish, Polish, and German, but mainly Swedish. Another precedes everything he says with "I don't mean to be an asshole, but . . ." If they are confounded by the presence of oranges in a ball bucket, then I truly do not know what this world is coming to, except of course we all do know: a reckoning. Which is why we had better work on our appreciation of oranges.

First of all, they are a bright and sunshiny orange, that eternal happy marriage of red and yellow. Second of all, you can make a funny smile by putting a section of orange peel in your mouth. You can't fake an orange-peel smile. Then there's the juice. A wise man who lives in Round Rock, Texas, once told me, "Any day gets better when you drink orange juice." This is one of the smartest things anyone has ever said to me, up there with "Happy wife, happy life," which I gleaned from marriage counseling, and "I care too much," which a wise woman from Kansas City once told me is the correct answer to the job-interview question "What are your flaws?"

I do care too much — about oranges. My dad liked orange juice. After drinking it, he would say, "Ahh," then smile his secret smile. I can't describe this smile — it's a secret — but I can tell you that sunlight travels through outer space until it hits an orange tree, which turns that light into an orange, so when you drink orange juice, what's hitting you is energy from the sun.

All energy is like that, but people don't like to talk about it. People prefer being miserable.

Another wise man, this one from St. Louis, once told me the problem with people is we lack the vocabulary to say what we like about things; it's easier to complain and be negative.

Take my teammates. They think oranges and baseballs are so unalike that they don't belong together in a bucket. C'mon. They're both round and fun to hit with a bat. (You have to suck the juice out of the orange first, though. Otherwise you're wasting food, which my mom taught me is wrong.) But even if oranges and baseballs had nothing whatsoever in common, why can't they be in a bucket together? We have got to get over our differences, people.

3

The orange tree in my backyard is like the desert sky on a clear night: all you see are stars, except the stars are oranges, more than I can count without getting lost, more than I can eat. Which brings me to the question: Will a food bank take my extra backyard oranges? I ask my period-three students, and Leda, the first person in my fashion experience to herald the return of the leopard print, immediately replies,

"SOVA." That's the Jewish food pantry on the west side of LA, where you'd go to get a mezuzah or to attend Orthodox services. I head over to SOVA with a box and a shopping bag full of oranges I've picked.

The guy at SOVA says he will have to weigh the fruit, which is pretty exciting, to put a number on that infinity of oranges. He has long, straight white hair and a narrow, unemotional face, as if he has seen things and also read books. While he's in the back, I look around and see that the pantry is very neat: not a crumb in sight, all the cans and boxes lined up nicely.

The guy returns and announces, "Thirty-seven pounds." I think, Wow. A woman, also with long, straight white hair, emerges from the back and says, "It's a good thing you came, because we're out of fruit." I think, Double-wow. Here I am, donating oranges, doing some good. Grateful for the opportunity.

4

Two things happened at school yesterday that give me faith. First, Aisha came in during my conference period and asked if she could make orange juice. I keep a big bag of oranges and a cast-iron juicer in the classroom for this very purpose.

"Absolutely, go right ahead, please do," I told her, all three invitations at once, so eager was I for good-natured Aisha to fulfill my dream of students dropping by to squeeze oranges. She might have been motivated by the fact that my wife and I had gone to the soul-food restaurant in Inglewood that Aisha had recommended, on the very day she'd recommended it. If that's the case, then I say, Hooray for positive feedback loops, and double hooray for Aisha.

Her visit would have been enough to validate my faith in orange appreciation right there, but wait; there's more. Right after Aisha's visit,

I brought my ball bucket and bat and tee out to the schoolyard to get in some quick batting practice at lunch. We have a gigantic lawn here at our high school, with room for students to play soccer and to lie with their heads in one another's laps and to give piggyback rides — and for me to swat green plastic practice balls off the tee.

Dune sees me lugging my gear and calls out from across the yard, "Can I play?" This is another dream come true. Dune is a young man of many talents. For example, he can recognize what key a song is in just by hearing it. And he can talk to adults. I don't let him go first, though. This is my time. I hit a couple of feeble grounders to start, but those are just warm-ups; here come the solid line drives: soaring, splendid, yes.

Now it's Dune's turn. After he gets warmed up, he starts thwacking them to the opposite field: more soaring, more splendor. Dune and I, student and teacher, are playing ball together. What was I just saying about getting over our differences? It's happening, here and now.

Then Mona comes over. She's getting her batting practice in when all of a sudden Dune notices a couple of oranges in the bucket. I am standing in the outfield, poised to catch Mona's fly balls, too far away for conversation. Dune gestures to the oranges: question mark? I gesture back: exclamation point! He picks up an orange like he's won a prize, which he has: the orange appreciation award, on behalf of us all.

20

How I Got to First Base

My new black catcher's mitt still isn't broken in. To break it in, I have to pound the pocket with a special tool called a "glove mallet" — I don't know for how long. Until it's broken in, I suppose. I've had this mitt since a year ago last spring, and it's a work in progress. I pound it every so often but apparently not enough. Now that I have a deadline — tryouts for a new league are in six weeks, in February — I plan to be more disciplined.

The regimen: twenty-seven simulated pitches into the pocket, each with an angry-sounding *thwack*, the sound of "this far and no further." Twenty-seven: a perfect game, each batter striking out on three pitches … Wait a second. Math check: nine innings, three outs an inning, three strikes per out — I should be thwacking my mitt *eighty-one* times. No wonder it's not broken in yet. I must triple my efforts, re-creating the glory of snaring every pitch of a three-pitch-strikeout perfect game. What a sublime accomplishment that would be.

I wonder what the neighbors think I'm doing. They seem resigned to a certain ruckus from my office, where, when not pounding a mitt, I'm often blasting rock music loud enough to see the subwoofer shudder. If they can stand to hear me screaming along to "Father of Mine" by Everclear with my ultraheartfelt classic-rock gestures, they can stand the staccato thwacks of my pounding a glove.

I'd really like to get in a full season with this mitt. "For the PROFES-SIONAL player," it proclaims in silver lettering on the black leather. I am no more a PROFESSIONAL than a kid on a tricycle is a STOCK-CAR RACER. And that kid could conceivably grow up to become a stock-car racer, whereas I am two decades and counting past the end of all but the most enduring pro ballplayer's career; never mind being several orders of magnitude behind even a subaverage Major Leaguer in talent.

But so what? I can still play. And what would you rather I do? Crawl unburdened toward death, King Lear–style? Play golf? I think not. I plan to keep playing ball until one or both of my knees finally says, *This far and no further*, or I find something else to aspire to, such as enlightenment, a mystic connection to the divine — which is, in fact, part of my long-term plan, along with goat-herding along the banks of the Pedernales. But only after I can patently no longer squat for nine innings.

Some catchers will hustle up the first-base line on ground balls to back up the throw to first. I find this truly admirable. I myself send sincere best wishes up the first-base line, but getting up and down from the crouch is the extent of my range behind the plate. I'm confident, though, that I'll be able to hit line drives until I'm dead.

What I would like to do while still alive is throw a guy out at second base — the long toss, 120 feet, the hero's heave. Third base would be good, too, though it's possible there to overthrow and let the runner score. Risky, you say? Let's try it! Our lives are defined by the risks we take, or so I overheard a student say in the halls of the school where I teach.

I'm also up for picking a runner off at first. Point being I am sick of letting my opponents scamper around the bases unchallenged. That's why I am committed to a training program of hurling baseballs from the back-porch deck — across the milkweed, lavender, blackberries, and primrose — to the top of a batting net out by the grapefruit trees, near the compost heap. I just have to find and keep the correct arm motion:

overhead, not sidearm or three-quarters, as I have been throwing my entire life. This is manifestly still doable. On the wall I have my training regimen written on teal Post-Its:

Start with dart throws.

Hold at wrist.

Hold at elbow.

Get rid of elbow.

"Dart throws" means toss the ball like you're throwing a dart. "Hold at wrist" means do the dart throw while supporting the right wrist with your left hand. "Hold at elbow" means support the arm there, and don't give up no matter what. I don't remember what "Get rid of elbow" means. I got this training regimen from an Internet video. I suppose I could watch it again, but I feel like, at a certain point, you just have to figure these things out for yourself.

As I said, tryouts for the new league are six weeks away. The old league is too far from my Los Angeles neighborhood, and I also got a not-undeserved rap there for fighting with my teammates. They just say and do such Not Right things. For example, on my first team in that league, the guy ahead of me in the order, Curt, tried giving me batting tips while we waited our turns at the plate. Whatever. I blotted it out. Curt was our nimble infielder who sported a skullcap in the dugout, which gave him the appearance of being a rugged scholar of the game. It's a good look. Personally I don't have a large enough head to pull it off.

I would gladly have admired Curt if he hadn't been such a bad sport. He hollered at pitchers to "just throw strikes" and exuded exasperation loudly. Being a quietly encouraging person myself, I find flagrant negativity objectionable. Which is why I picked a fight with him.

He gave me his batting tips, whatever they were, and I let them smash into my indifference like poor little birdies into a plateglass window. Then Curt strode to the plate and struck out on three consecutive pitches, flailing more pathetically with each missed swing. Surging with schadenfreude, I got up next and blooped a first-pitch single to the opposite field. The ball took a hard right on the bounce, evading a flabbergasted outfielder who otherwise would have easily thrown me out at first. As it was, I plodded determinedly down the baseline and arrived safely, at which point I was wisely replaced with a pinch runner. After my joyous trundle back to the dugout, I shared with Curt my heartfelt thoughts on the value of his batting tips: "Don't … give … me … ad … vice," I told him. It was all I could get out after that frenzied dash to first.

Curt took this flagrant showboating the way a fuse takes a flame. "We've got some real prima donnas on this team," he huffed.

Huff all you want, big fella. You heard me. Thus spake my body language as I positioned myself at the far end of the dugout and studied the lead being taken by my pinch runner. I'd like to say my teammates congratulated me on my bloop single, and perhaps they did, though mildly, as it truly was not much of a hit. One click up from a walk, no big deal; we won't speak of it again. I was too focused on what Curt was saying at the other end of the dugout. I couldn't make out the particulars, but there was a lot of huffing and puffing, and it felt like time to blow the house down.

So I observed, with the sort of condescension that has been rankling my opponents and teammates alike since Little League, "It sounds like you're upset, Curt. Would you like to discuss your feelings?"

To which he replied that I was a "washed-up has-been." (My teammates were all thirty years younger than I was.) To which I replied that his statement was redundant. At which point he came charging, and our teammates intervened.

Nobody really wants the token old man on the team to be picking fights in the dugout. My teammates shook their heads while the manager put a firm arm across my shoulders and led me up the left-field line for a talk. I was supposed to feel chastened, but instead I felt like the grand marshal of a pent-up-aggression parade, waving to an adoring crowd of kindred souls also tired of playing nice.

The manager, who in his other, not-baseball, life was either a stock-broker or a bail bondsman, had the sober demeanor of a person who might not always act with sobriety but understood the role to be played here. He wanted my assurance that This Was Over.

"Most definitely," I told him. I had said what I wanted to say.

"Not the time for it," he reiterated.

"It's not like I'm going to see him during the week," I countered, apparently not finished after all. He looked at me skeptically, and I looked at him like a man with nothing to lose. If I was going to back down, I would have done it already. The manager was a decent guy, committed to winning. He had way better catchers than me on the roster, as any manager committed to winning would.

So there we stood for a little while, and a little bit longer still. I felt peaceful, with no want or need for justification. Eventually, for the sake of the game, I agreed to shake Curt's hand, which was all the manager wanted to hear.

I victory-ambled back to the dugout, where Curt left me hanging with my hand out. No surprise there. Who was the bigger man now? Never have I felt the sun shine more benevolently upon me than I did in that moment with my hand extended and Curt not understanding the role to be played. That was on him.

What was on me was the lesson to be learned: not to pick fights with teammates. Yet the next season, when I was starting catcher for the worst club in the league, I had a bat-throwing, glove-hurling lout on my team. Let's call him Louty. His bat never actually hit anyone, and when he hurled his glove to the ground after a routine error, his poor sportsmanship made the rest of us feel like jolly good fellows. Our role was to assure him that it was OK to strike out with runners on base time after time.

That was all fine, but what's never fine is ignoring "I got it." People can and do get hurt — *I've* gotten hurt — when one guy calls for a pop fly and some lunatic comes charging in to catch it anyway. Louty was that lunatic. I kept my distance for the first half of the season, but you remember how I really can't abide negativity? Well, it turns out I also can't abide flagrant disregard of "I got it." Basically hit REPEAT on my dustup with Curt, and you'll see half the team pushing me away from Louty, who was being pushed by the other half in the opposite direction. The only difference this time was that we did shake hands afterward.

And now I'm looking for a new team in a new league, preferably one where I don't feel compelled to fight my own teammates over common baseball decency.

Or so I was when I started this essay, back when I was working on breaking in my catcher's mitt and improving my throwing accuracy, when tryouts were still six weeks away.

I was writing this to psych myself up to find a new team where I would not be known as a dugout brawler. And I did, in fact, get on with a team I loved, this time in a thirty-five-and-older league, meaning there were actually some players within a decade of me. We were the Athletics, which is perfect because I have the Oakland A's in my DNA. Atop my dresser at home is a picture from 1988 of my friend Jimmy and me sporting full-body smiles in the press box at the Oakland Coliseum. We had wrangled press passes under the auspices of writing loosey-goosey baseball commentary for an alternative weekly. Earlier that same afternoon All-Star slugger Dave "The Cobra" Parker had revealed to me the secret of hitting: "Hit the fucker hard, and hope it goes far." I keep this revelation enshrined in the same chamber of my heart where my rabbinical ancestors kept their favorite Scriptures.

If I am ever going to stick with any team, it's this one. I didn't even have to try out. The manager picked me on the basis of a phone interview. We were talking baseball philosophy, and I said there is nothing else in life like standing in the batter's box; it is the truest of all moments of truth. He said, "Stop right there. You're in."

In our first practice game he had me starting behind the plate and batting cleanup, too. I smacked a line drive up the middle in my first at bat, which quickly settled my batting position. But after seeing me behind the plate for three innings — my catcher's mitt, despite all that thumping, still not broken in — he asked how I felt about playing first base.

I agreed with alacrity. First base is where aging catchers go. Also I had started feeling a stabbing pain in my left knee — not constantly, but often enough. It hurt so much I would shout, "Ouch!" and the knee often buckled. The time had come for me to get up from the crouch.

First base turned out to be not so horrible. I made a few nifty scoops with a beat-up old fielder's mitt. My teammates seemed sincerely supportive. One of them did comment, "Well, of course — he's a catcher!" You know you're on the right team when the other players make you feel good about yourself.

After four games I was hitting .375 and feeling confident that I could maintain that above-average average for the foreseeable future, when the pandemic ended the season. Being over .300 helped me cope with the cancellation of baseball and pretty much everything else.

In the unlimited interim I have staple-gunned two aluminum pie plates to the top of the blackberry trellis. When hit with a ball, they give a satisfying *clack-clack*. My goal is to hit them three times in a row. I'm currently good for about one out of four. I like the challenge.

I have also developed a new throwing theory that involves lining up the bulging bunion of my left foot so that it points toward the pie pans. This, I imagine, opens up my hips, something I always read about in interviews with pitching coaches. And I have had plenty of time to read here amid the pandemic, which is like a long and deadly rain delay.

Lately I've been thinking about the rest of my catcher's equipment. Precious as it is, what would make it even more precious would be to give it away. I bet the Boys & Girls Club of Venice will snap it up, once it's safe to play baseball again. I'll give them everything: helmet, mask, chest protector, shin guards, the equipment bag itself. If this sounds like the bargaining phase of grief, that's just about right.

The only thing I'll keep is the mitt, which I'm still breaking in, this time as a pillow for the sadness that keeps me up at night. It works only sometimes. One day, when the mitt is finally broken in and the pandemic is over, I'll play catch with anyone who still wants to play.

21

The Gift is to the Giver

Hardball, not softball. That's how I have always defined myself, until now. Hitting a baseball now is still fun, but the truth is that actually playing baseball, as in suiting up and showing up for a four-hour game on a Sunday morning – that is no longer fun.

I learned this while benchwarming last season, dedicating time I could have been gardening or playing tennis or hanging out with my wife, to instead batting alternate-11th, which means every two hours or so I got an at-bat. The rest of the time I sat behind home plate on a cement slab with the other benchwarmers.

One of them was a Los Angeles Fire Department captain, now retired and battling long COVID. After several weeks of us sitting next to each other, rooting for our guys and razzing the opponents, I asked him if he had been there back in 1986 for the Central Library fire, which I know about because Susan Orlean writes about bookshelf combustion so grippingly in *The Library*. I thought that if I could draw my benchmate out on the subject, it might lead in the direction of friendship.

"It was an unfightable fire," he said, looking into an unseeable distance. "All you could do was watch."

And that was that. He kept the box score while the other benchwarmers and I competed for roles such as warming up the pitcher when the catcher was still getting on his gear; or worse, warming up the left fielder; or worst of all, chasing down foul balls. The other, nimbler benchwarmers nabbed those assignments, leaving me to gaze beyond the outfield fence at the extremely eroded slopes of the San Gabriel Mountains.

"What do you think, mountains?" I would frequently ask. "Should I quit?"

The mountains always answered, "No, stick it out, this team is going to go all the way to the championship and we want you to be there, as opposed to moving away, going on vacation or deciding to quit-- as you have on every other team you've ever played on that went to the championship."

I used this oracular pronouncement as bedrock upon which to form my final baseball identity of Not-A-Quitter. I took quiet pride in this identity, but even after taking quiet pride, that still left two hours before my next at-bat, so I would use the mountains as a backdrop to project my career highlights.

There I am as an eight-year-old, chasing balls my otherwise reliable and accurate father hurled over my head. His dad only played catch with him once, being otherwise too busy safeguarding his wife and five children through the Great Depression. As a kid, I was lucky to be chasing after balls my own dad took time and interest to hurl over my head and off to the right.

Look! That's me, quitting Little League at age 14 because the manager didn't take to my sarcasm. And there I am not playing baseball again until I'm 30, about to become a dad myself. It's the championship game of the Los Angeles Baseball Association – the one championship game I do play in -- and my team is winning by a run, the opposing team at bat in the bottom of the ninth with two outs, bases loaded. I'm playing third base, thinking "Hit-it-to-me, hit-it-to-me," an incantation against dread that the batter actually will hit it to me, which he does, which turns out fine because I snag that grounder and now all I have to do is step on third and we win the championship.

But instead it's not fine, because I hurl the ball at the catcher, over his head and to the right. Hence, we do not win the championship. I have been on other teams that did win the championship, but never with me present. I always seem to have moved away, gone on vacation or to have quit the team by then.

I do have successful highlights. I went 3-for-4 in an All-Star game, three line drive singles to center field, my specialty. I was also featured in a news report on national television, playing catcher, rolling the ball back to the mound after our female pitcher, who was playing in a professional women's baseball league, struck out a guy for out number three.

And once, as I stepped up to bat, I heard an infielder warn, "Line drive hitter!" Admittedly, this was while playing softball, but still, it's engraved on my plaque at the Baseball Hall of Fame in Cooperstown, New York.

I took pride in never asking the manager last season why I wasn't playing. He had either adapted a curmudgeonly persona or was in fact a curmudgeon. Either way, he wasn't going to tell me he was saving me for the right situation. There was no right situation. I'm 60. My knees hurt. I didn't want to quit, but benchwarming gave me time to think and finally come to realize that the affirmation I seek from baseball is not so much about playing a full nine-inning game as it is about as tossing a ball up and hitting it. Also, it doesn't have to be a ball. It can be a fallen orange.

That's actually better. When you barrel up on a fallen orange, the air smells citrus-y. And you don't have to hasten global warming by driving out 20 miles to the ball field on a Sunday morning. I can stand in my backyard and swat balls and oranges out of sight. This is what I love, when the batted object soars over the lemon tree, through the sycamore leaves, over the red-flowered Tecoma vines, never to be seen again.

It reminds me of summer vacation last summer, at a campsite just outside of Boulder, Colorado. There I played Wiffle ball against a six-year-old who jumped out to a quick lead on pure scrappiness, which I admired. I came storming back on a pair of towering home runs way up into the tall, tall pines. It's true -- the ball carries further at altitude.

Taking that scrappy six-year-old kid majestically deep, fairy-tale deep --
that is the hardest I have laughed during all of COVID. If that kid ever
grows up and somehow reads this – I wasn't laughing at you, kid. I was
laughing from pleasure in being alive. And besides, don't forget -- in the
end, you won.

Hitting a ball so far that it disappears: that is the glory. It goes back
to earliest childhood, being a little baby who learns to close his eyes to
make everything go away. Press your pudgy little baby palms right into
your eye sockets to feel the joy of pulsating inside-the-head stars.

You could call this pleasure infantile. I prefer to think of it as primal.
To better connect with my batting self, I recently made a stick figure
statue of myself at bat, using pipe cleaners and popsicle sticks. I did this
together with my high school students as an exercise for writing college
entrance essays. Yes, I'm a high school English teacher, retiring at the
end of this school year, which is another reason why I am thinking so
much these days about reaching the end of doing something you love.

According to my lesson plan, the pipe cleaner statues are action
figures of ourselves at our best, showing leadership or creativity or over-
coming challenges. Ideally, the figurines are not only calming to work
on while we're clustered at school together amid a raging pandemic,
but they also give us ideas for vivid verbs and gripping sensory details.
This very essay I am crafting for you right now began as an example of
a college application essay describing an element of your identity that is
so meaningful your application would be incomplete without it.

This essay would be incomplete without me telling you how much
I love my stick figure batter's deep crouch. *He* can keep his knees bent
forrrrrrevvvverrr. I also love his arms, aloft. He is perpetually poised;
his cotton puff head, focused. He is my dream come true. Now that
I have officially stuck it out as a benchwarmer and been there for the
championship game and got my picture taken holding the trophy –both
Marko and the trophy gleaming, this picture is my all-time greatest
social media like-getter -- I have quit my team and bid playing a fond
farewell.

This gives me more time for kale. Kale is coming up in rows in my garden – not just scattered wherever, as has been my gardening technique for years -- but in neat rows and lots of 'em. I'm going to have enough kale to give away to food banks.

I also have more time for tennis. I am on a team tennis team, and the manager greeted me at our last practice by pressing his hands together, nodding, and saying, "Sensei." What an honor!

I asked him yesterday for advice about volleying. I feel ready to pounce at the net but this readiness does not consistently manifest in winners. On the contrary. Despite my loosey-goosiness, when I volley, the ball often crumples forlornly into the net.

My manager heard me and replied, "You're a baseball player, right?"
I said yes.

"Try catching the volley. People think you have to clobber the ball, but all you have to do is catch it on your racquet."

"I played catcher," I said, feeling the pulse of life, the way it runs extra-strongly within when you feel your identity has been recognized, acknowledged, and affirmed. It is my hope that you, faithful non-quitting reader, will have a spoken exchange with someone, soon, that will be equivalently life-affirming.

Meanwhile, to bring this essay home, let me end by sharing that I have reused and recycled my stick figure-at-the-bat. A quiet student, who does her work and has indicated through her writing that she really cares about reading, doubled back after class was over to ask me in the doorway if I please happened to have any extra pipe cleaners she could borrow because she is making a stop-motion video.

I told her, let's see what we can find.

Mark Gozonsky's first published writing appeared the summer before his Bar Mitzvah in *The San Antonio Jewish Journal.* He has since published in *The New York Times, The Sun,* and *Lit Hub.* He is currently at work on his next book, about his quest to play tennis on every free public court in Los Angeles, where he lives with his wife.